# Industry Thought Leaders Praise
# *Managing Sales Leads*

I've known Jim Obermayer for close to 20 years. Jim is, without doubt, the number one expert in the area of lead generation, lead management, and literally all aspects of the science of finding prospects that are interested in buying your products. His new book will help the reader develop and implement a systematic approach to generating high quality, profitable leads.

**Gilbert E. Cargill**
**CEO, Cargill Consulting Group**

Finally, a book that gives the **facts** for "sales engine" success by showing marketing what they need to do to serve the sales organization! "Managing Sales Leads" shows you the procedures and numbers required to meet your quotas through defined lead generation and management metrics, leading to accurate forecasting. Regardless of the talent of your sales team, this is a sales and marketing blueprint for understanding their true capability and a factual basis for holding them accountable to sales objectives and goals.

**John B. Hasbrouck**
**President and CEO**
**NewLeads, Inc.**

I have been waiting for a book like this for a long time. Whether you are just starting a lead management system or you want to make your existing process more effective, Jim Obermayer's, *Managing Sales Leads* is the one resource that offers everything you need.

From designing a lead management process, to justifying a new and improved lead management system, to presenting an airtight case for a lead management system, this book covers it all. It will help you generate more sales.

**Matthew Hill**
**President, The Hill Group**


Generating sales leads and the management of those leads is the true test of marketing ROI. Jim Obermayer is one of the few who not only understands that but makes it easy for the rest of us to comprehend. And this is the book that clearly maps out the entire process from start to finish for beginner and pro alike. If you're at all concerned about getting more prospects, turning more of them into customers, and improving your Marketing ROI, you must read this book.

**Rick Kean**
**Former Executive Director, Business Marketing Association**
**President, The Business Marketing Institute**

Finally, someone hit the nail on the head. If you want to know the real inside strategies used by successful marketers to managing sales leads from someone who's been in the field and seen what works and what doesn't, read this book NOW!

**Russell Kern**
**Founder/CEO, The Kern Organization.**
**Author,** *S.U.R.E. Fire Direct Response Marketing*


Executives today are tired of marketing efforts wasting their company's valuable resources. In *Managing Sales Leads*, Obermayer provides a measurable method of marketing guaranteed to gain market share at an extraordinary and predictable rate.

**Pamela Wasley**
**CEO/President**
**Cerius Consulting**

# Managing Sales Leads

*Turning Cold Prospects into Hot Customers*

JAMES OBERMAYER

**Managing Sales Leads: Turning Cold Prospects into Hot Customers**
James W. Obermayer

Library of Congress Cataloging in Publication Number is available. See page 256 for details.

For more information about our products, contact us at:

Thomson Learning Academic Resource Center
1-800-423-0563

**Thomson Higher Education**
5191 Natorp Boulevard
Mason, Ohio 45040
USA

# Contents

# Introduction

Properly managing sales leads is the only true tool to measure marketing's successful contribution to sales. Without a system which promotes measurement and discipline, salespeople flounder, prospects are left uncalled, and marketing can't prove the ROI for the money entrusted to their care. While this book covers the "How-To" aspects of managing inquiries, it spends a considerable amount of time on the real reasons why after over 200 years this basic discipline of attending to the inquirers needs is still floundering.

On the wall of my office hangs a page from the Evansville Daily Journal, Monday Morning, June 28th, 1857. It is framed so that both sides of the page can be read and viewed. My original interest in the page is that my mother's family (The Lynxwilers) were said to be some of the original settlers in the Evansville, Indiana, area (really a few miles north in a town called Newburgh).

The page has interesting stories about "River Intelligence," which describes boats and ferries coming and going to the Evansville Port and all of the goods that will be on the boats. There is a story of horse thieves caught and hung, "Telegraphic" announcements of news from the east (big ice storms in Washington, DC, on June 21, 1857 and New York City on June 22, 1857), riots in Detroit on June 22 (six houses of ill repute were stormed and the inhabitants thrown into the street; only one person stabbed). Most of these pages have advertisements. I am struck by the plethora of ads which hawk everything from buttons to ice, whiskey to clothing, 200 sacks of nice white corn, glassware (18 dozen assorted tumblers) and new books (Longfellow's new poems, prose and the new editions of Waverly novels, the most elegant library edition ever published—only $0.75 per volume). There is even an advertisement for the Royal Havana Lottery sponsored by the Spanish government for $300,000 in prizes to be held on July 7, 1857.

In tiny type the advertising promises shout from the page using borrowed interest headlines or simple declarations of available goods. There were calls to action, but in those days there were no telephone numbers, Web addresses, coupons or BRCs, just an address as to where the goods could be found. The proprietor's name appears and on some an address (Fairbanks Scales available at Hornbrook & Co., General Agents, Water Street, Evansville). It was enough to announce that a product was available and the people could find the proprietor.

As I read these pages from my great, great grandfathers' past, I realize how little things have changed in the last 147 years. The proprietor of I & D Heimann Grocers (Main Street two doors back of second) could only tell if advertising worked if the goods came off the shelves and if Mr. Heimann asked people who bought, "did you see my advertisements in the June 28th paper?" In those days it was walk-in traffic or advertisements. The sellers either knew the ads worked when new people came in the day the ad ran or they didn't. It was simple.

Today advertising has taken many new forms. With the multiplication of advertising opportunities and the explosion of distribution channels, finding out which marketing dollar gives you the best yield is not easy. While the sales are not substantially different from 150 years ago, an advertisers ability to prove the return on investment has also not gotten too much better for most companies. They still judge advertising and it's related promotional cousin of direct marketing by the amount of product that leaves the shelves rather than the exact number of people who respond to advertising and can be tracked as buyers. Back in the Evansville days of June 1857 there was probably one newspaper in town and that was easy to track for those that advertised. But later, when more newspapers appeared and billboards and radio and even advertisement by mail (direct marketing) were introduced, it became more difficult to know which advertisement gave the advertiser the best results, and which ad didn't.

That is what this book is all about: how to determine which advertisement (generic for any marketing dollars spent to create a preferred product interest) works by feeding the salespeople with the names of prospects and getting results reported back to you so that future decisions on promotions are better than past decisions. Without this basic knowledge, of who bought from which source of advertising, marketing is no better than it was in June of 1857.

And this is the crime of it all. Marketing creates tremendous wealth but it seldom gets credit because it lacks the will or the know-how to prove the ROI for it's efforts. This can only be accomplished if there is an inquiry management system in place, with the full cooperation of sales and marketing. Hence, the reason for this work.

A special thank you must go to several people who materially contributed to this book. Dick Evans, founder of AdTrack Corporation, read and helped me work through the best practices recommendations throughout this work. His comments prodded and poked, guided and questioned many concepts and ideas that needed questioning. Susan Obermayer, my spouse and former sales representative, was an equal in questioning many of the recommendations in this work. Russell Kern of The Kern Organization discussed with me at length his thoughts about inquiry qualification and the inquiry stages with the sales and marketing process. Richard Hagle, publisher of my previous two books, and of hundreds of other books, has been especially patient as this work came together.

SECTION ONE **Making the Case**

# 1 Sue Makes the Sale

The following scene is being played out more and more often in companies today.

The situation in the company was simple. No one was making quota. Spending on marketing was at an all-time low as budgets were slashed to make up for a decline in volume and lost profits. The marketing manager moved on when his meager budget disappeared and the business press about the company turned sour. Sue, a new marketing manager, was hired to "fix" things.

---

The executive team was meeting to consider an increase in the marketing department's budget. It was a million dollar commitment, and the argument revolved around return on investment.

"How soon will we begin to see a payback from Sue's marketing plan?" George, the CFO, demanded. "Can we expect a 10 or 20 times return?"

Cynthia, the VP of Engineering, asked, "And how long will it take? Why give marketing the money? I haven't seen a break-even timetable much less a 10 or 20 times return."

Daniel, the company President, held up his hand to quiet those around the table and turned to Steven, the Marketing VP, who Sue worked for, and asked, "What does she tell you when you ask her these questions, Steve?"

"She tells me," he grimaced, "that we'll get at least a 20% return on our marketing investment. We have to spend this amount just to be competitive—irrespective of return."

George chimed in, "Look, we gave manufacturing a million and a half bucks a year ago for that machinery purchase, and, right on target, within six months of installation, we recouped the purchase price. From the seventh month on we've netted a 20% increase in productivity, which has reduced our cost of goods."

"And don't forget," Cynthia said, "the new software has lived up to its promise of reducing the engineering time spent on new product designs, and we have been able to bring products to market much faster than we did several years ago. "

"So the question still stands," Daniel said, looking down the long boardroom table: "If we give Sue the million dollars she is asking for marketing, what will our break-even point be and can she guarantee at least a 20% ROI?" And then, almost as an after thought, but with a stern, pleading tone of voice, he said, "I'd rather have a 35% return, Steven. If not, we should just let the product sell itself as it has in the past."

"I have an idea," Cynthia said, with undisguised glee in her voice. "Let's call Sue and have her plead her case for the million she wants."

And with that, Steve reluctantly picked up the phone and dialed Sue's office. Hoping that she was out and maybe the confrontation could be put off until they could make a better case, Steve was just starting to feel relieved by the fourth ring when Sue answered the phone.

"Eh, Sue, this is Steve. We're all sitting here in the executive boardroom going over your budget request, and frankly we need more clarification on the payback. If you don't have time now to do it, can we set a time for you in the next few weeks?" He listened for a minute or so, while the others around the table started to smile at the thought of permanently tabling the marketing budget. "Oh, you can come down now?" he smiled. "Yes, we have a projector already set up. Twenty minutes? Yes, we can do that."

Steve looked around the table and suggested that they take a 20-minute break to allow Sue to get set up. With the nods from those around the table, Steve excused himself and went to Sue's office to discuss what he had gotten them into.

"Of course I'm ready," she said, closing her laptop. "I thought I was due to present the numbers next week. Why did it come up now?" With an exasperated voice Steve mumbled something to the effect that word had gotten out about her budget and how it was brought up in the staff meeting, and how one thing leads to another.

"That's OK," Sue said with a mischievous smile. "It's time we showed them what's on our minds and why. I wanted to show you the numbers before they got wind of it. But what the heck, it should be a good show. You do trust me, don't you?"

"Why yes," Steve said. "We're due in the conference room in a few minutes, so let's get going."

## The Marketing Manager Presents Her Plan

Sue started up the PowerPoint presentation, smiled, and launched into the preamble of the Marketing budget. "This year," she said, "we're going to accelerate our market growth. And while you see the usual allocations for collateral materials, Web site upgrades, market research, support tools, and specialty items, the big difference this year is the proactive go-to-market plan we will implement in order to generate sales. The million dollars of incremental budget I am requesting is for pure down-and-dirty-lead generation. We will increase the total number of inquiries and, consequently, qualified leads by 300%. Sales will begin to show increases within 90 to 180 days."

Sue looked about the room from one manager to the next and said, "This year I am going to find the buyers and not rely on them finding us. Our products can't sell themselves when no one knows we exist. I am taking on a quota for both lead generation and sales."

It was at this point that George couldn't help himself. He launched into a nonstop burst: "I thought only Sales had a quota and what kind of a quota are you talking about and how are you going to be measured and are you really thinking you can prove some kind of ROI from these marketing dollars and is it at least a 30% return and how are you going to do this because no one else has ever done it at the company in *my* 20 years?" "After all," he said with a gasp and a smile, "our products have always sold themselves; we didn't need anything but literature and to go to a few shows." By this time George was out of breath.

Sue smiled back and said, "Let me show you how it will be done."

Sue had started to make waves from her first week with the company. Management thought they knew who they were hiring, but there was almost immediate uneasiness within the company. Some people began connecting Sue's name with "change," "marketing responsibility," and "marketing quotas." Yet the salespeople she met liked what they heard when she used words such as "gap closure," "results acceleration," "cost drivers," "cause-and-effect analysis," "qualified sales leads," "increased pipeline velocity," "business case formulas," "promotional windows," "sales lead quotas," and "marketing accountability."

For three months she traveled with salespeople, grilled the sales staff on their quotas, and met with her product managers and marketing communications staff behind closed doors. She was planning for the coming year she said, but some people were of the opinion she was plotting—plotting to make changes and disrupt their way of doing things. Once when confronted by one of the disgruntled product managers about changing the way things had been done in the past, she responded, "It's precisely why I was hired—to break you away from doing things the way they have always been done and help the salespeople make quota for the first time in three years." That shut everyone up and put the word out that Sue meant business. Change was in the air.

Marketing's spending in the past had never been high on the list of "must-do's" of senior management, which came from the engineering ranks. In their world the product sold itself with only minimal support from marketing. After all, the company president believed, salespeople were only marginally necessary and the marketing staff rated below sales. It was the "accountability thing," he was fond of saying. These marketing types talked about creativity, branding, and positioning, but they couldn't tell him what he was getting in return for the dollars he gave them. Every time he hired someone in marketing he found that they had some "budget requirements" of a few hundred thousand dollars. When he asked what he got in return, there were blank stares and indignant responses:

- "But this is marketing. I can't give you an ROI."
- "Marketing isn't measured that way."
- "We don't have tools to measure marketing's contribution to sales; you just have to trust us."

- "It takes years for marketing's contributions to show up, and the salespeople won't give us credit."
- "Sales doesn't tell us what happened to the leads."

So, the President, like presidents everywhere, accepted the rhetoric and the excuses, while at the same time minimizing the money given to marketing. "If they can't prove their contributions beyond pretty collateral, a Web presence, a few trade shows, and some advertisements," Daniel had said last year, "I'll give them the minimum, hire the minimum staff, and, when times are tight, cut their budgets first. When times are good, we don't need to spend much on marketing. After all: Our products sell themselves."

So this is what Sue faced when she looked down the table that day. But she knew going into this job what the challenge would be. She had dealt with this type of thinking in the past. Actually, it was harder, she knew, to turn the sales types around because of their innate self-reliance.

In the next hour Sue presented her marketing plan with sales quotas by product, objectives, strategies, tactics, time frame of implementation, and budget. She showed the number of "inquiries" required by product, qualified leads by product, by month, and by quarter. Sharing her formulas for projecting the number of inquiries needed to make quota, she backed up the projections with other formulas showing the sales return from a block of inquiries. One issue she had to resolve, she said, was the inquiry management tracking system. Without a proper system in place she could not possibly know which of the many lead-generating tactics she was recommending were actually creating sales. With the proper system in place, she said, she would know the sales contribution level and whether she would be able to attain a 20% to a 40% return on the lead generation budget.

"Wait a minute," Cynthia interrupted. "Are you proposing that you will be able to track the individual contribution of an advertisement, a show, a direct mail campaign, and even our PR?"

Sue nodded and smiled, "Why would I ask you to give me money if I couldn't give you a predictable return on investment? I'm not shooting craps in Vegas. If you give me a dollar, it's my responsibility to predict and deliver an agreed-upon return on investment."

At this point Daniel, the President, jumped in, "But Sue, the sales reps close the sales. How will you know the results?"

Within a few minutes Sue showed them how the inquiry management system would work: It was the responsibility of sales to report on the disposition of every inquiry entrusted to their care. A sales inquiry is an asset of the company, she said, and it begins to decline in value from the minute it is created. It is a race between us and our competitors to solve the needs of the prospect. Inquiries are sales opportunities. If we don't follow up 100% of the inquiries, she said, we would not participate in 100% of the sales opportunities. The follow-up of sales inquiries, she found out, had been only 25%.

"When you give me this budget," she said, "it will take two years to reap the full sales return. But we will track each inquiry given to our salespeople. We'll credit the lead-generating sources with the sales that they produce for us. I will get rid of those magazine advertisements, shows, direct mail lists, and seminars that don't produce for us. I will be increasingly able to spend our money on the most productive lead-generation tactics. With the right information and these processes in place."

With those words still hanging in the room, the executives looked at each other. First one nodded, then the next and the next. As the company president finished his silent poll of the room, he said, "You've got your money. Get the inquiry management system in place and deliver."

---

How real is this? Several critical ideas (rules that follow later in the book) are very real and will be the focus of the rest of this book. They will be outlined in the next two chapters, and their implications will be explored and expanded upon. First is the "Rule of 45." Then there is recognition of a sales lead as a wasting asset. Finally, there is the 100% Imperative: the absolute requirement that sales reps follow up every single sales inquiry and that marketing is 100% responsible for the money it spends to furnish leads to the sales force.

In short, this book is about spending money on the "right"

targets and ignoring the rest. It's about directing salespeople to the most likely buyers to help them make quota. It's about how to account for, spend, and prove the ROI for the marketing and sales budgets that make up 10% to 30% of your company's yearly revenue. It's about all of these things plus the need to have a sales lead-tracking system, business rules, teamwork, and a service or software package that can make the growth engine hum, not chug, to the finish line every year. And lastly it's about proving the ROI for every lead generation tactic. The rest of this book will explore these ideas in depth.

Here are a few terms you've seen already or will see shortly:

- ROI (return on investment): How much money is returned to you for an investment.
- Wasting Asset: An asset whose value decreases over time.
- Did You Buy study: A study to determine whether or not an inquirer actually made a purchase.
- Lead/Inquiry(er): Someone who asks for more information about a product or product line.
- 100% Imperative: You must follow up 100% of leads to ensure maximum marketing ROI.
- Rule of 45: 45% of all inquirers will buy a product from someone within 12 months or less.

Note these terms when you see them. They might be the source of salvation for your company and your career.

# 2 Business Rules to Live By

As I discussed in the Introduction, sales and marketing departments are out of control because basic processes are not being applied consistently to fundamental business issues, the key among them being sales and marketing accountability. But, however you phrase it, billions of dollars of investment are being wasted, and billions more in lost opportunities are being squandered.

The first step is to understand the value of the sales lead assets being created. This can only happen if you understand the Rule of 45 and how to use it. Only then can you know how to predict a return on investment so that you can report on the results.

## The Rule of 45: How to Predict the Future

The Rule of 45 is the basic premise from which you can measure the effectiveness of virtually all lead generation programs.[1] It is a steady, reliable benchmark number that, simply stated, says that 45% of all inquirers will buy *someone's* product. The percentage of that group that buys your products is equal to your own market share. I have been involved in over 100 Did You Buy studies on a variety of products, and the Rule of 45 has consistently been proven, regardless of product (In the simplest terms, a Did You

Buy study is a study that asks prospects and inquirers "did you buy." More on this later.)

If you follow up 100% of the inquiries, the biggest variable in this formula is the time frame needed to reach the 45% threshold. For large-ticket items (over $100,000) the time to conversion can be as long as 18 months (sometimes longer), but for the great majority of products a one-year time frame is accurate. For products under $1,000 the inquiry conversion to a sale may be shorter and the conversion ratio higher (especially on business-to-consumer inquiries). See Exhibit 2.1.

On average the following rules-of thumb apply:

- Within three months 10% to 15% of business-to-business prospects will buy someone's product.

---

**EXHIBIT 2.1**
**The Rule of 45: Predicting Sales from a Particular Group of Inquiries**

Formula:

Inquiries x 45% x

Follow-up % x

Estimated Market Share % x

Average sales price (ASP) = Sales

Example:

1000 Inquiries x

45% x = 450 x

100% Follow-up = 450 x

25% Market share = 112 x

$10,000 ASP = $1,120,000 in Sales

Note: Numbers are rounded.

---

- Within six months 26% will buy someone's product.
- Within one year 45% will buy someone's product.

The decision to buy one product over another has more to do with follow-up by salespeople than any other single variable. After all, if you don't show up, you can't compete in the sales process.

As you view research from various sources that discuss the subject of conversion ratios of sales inquiries, you will run into varying statistics. Time frames, quality of inquiry, and other factors can influence specific outcomes, but regardless of variations, the inquiry closing ratios are predictable within a relatively tight range.

While 45% of the total inquirers will buy, this does not mean 45% of the qualified leads you receive will buy from you. The percentage that buy from you will depend on one of the great frustrating variables: sales lead follow-up by the sales force. Follow-up of the inquiry by finicky salespeople can make the difference between presenting to only 10% to 25% of the available buyers and presenting to 80% to 100% of the available buyers. Sales lead follow-up has always been the largest uncontrollable—or, more precisely, uncontrolled—variable.

How important is it to control this "invariable variable?" The following example shows lost revenue for a group of 100 inquirers with only a 25% follow-up.

There are 100 inquiries for a product with an average sales price of $10,000. If you want to know the total amount of product that will be sold from this group of inquiries, the formula is:

Inquiries × 45% × follow-up % × estimated market share % × average sales price = Sales

For example:
1000 inquiries × 45% = 450 potential buyers
 × 100% follow-up = 450 buyers
 × 25% market share = 112 buyers
 × ASP of $10,000 = $1,120,000 in Sales

Reduce the follow-up percentage to 50% and the inquiry sales yield drops to $560,000. Drop the follow-up to an average of 25%, and the sales yield drops to $280,000.

1000 Inquiries × 45% × **25%** FL-UP × 25% Mktsh
 × $10,000 ASP = $280,000

1000 Inquiries × 45% × **50%** FL-UP × 25% Mktsh
 × $10,000 ASP = $560,000

1000 Inquiries × 45% × **75%** FL-UP × 25% Mktsh
 × $10,000 ASP = $843,000

1000 Inquiries × 45% × **100%** FL-UP × 25% Mktsh
 × $10,000 ASP = $1,120,000

Of course, salespeople will say they have a sixth sense about sales inquiries and that they only follow up on the *real* buyers. If they were that good, they'd be at the racetrack—betting on the ponies and winning a lot of money. Nobody's instincts are *that* good.

## One Exception

There is one exception: It is possible to generate large quantities of inquiries that close below the 45% ratio. The reason for a lower closeout rate is most often due to using borrowed interest to solicit a larger-than-normal response, especially in direct marketing. For example, a company offered a free memory device to anyone who filled out a form, regardless of their need for the product. Of course, the response rate was far above the norm. The company's goal was to build a database with profile information as well as to find immediate-need buyers. They did both, but they created a lot of waste and "noise"—i.e., inquirers who were in no way going to buy their product and would simply be a waste of time following up.

The only way to get the total yield from your valid inquiries is to follow up 100% of them. If you do, you will gain market share at an exponential rate in comparison to your competitors (unless, of course, they are also following up 100% of their inquiries). If they only follow up 25% and you follow up and engage 100%, who will be the winner?

## Identifying Sources and Leads and Converting Them

The typical marketing manager wants to find sources of sales inquiries that will produce the most buyers. That manager looks for magazines that have the greatest number of buyers, lists that give the best response, and shows that have genuine buyers walking the floor. Once you have good sources and you know that you are finding the predictable percentage of inquirers who buy, you have to work on your own ability to convert a higher percentage of inquirers than your competitors.

If you have a response management system in place to measure the sales conversion of inquiries from a particular source, you will be in a position to consistently improve your ability to pick better and better sources for your sales leads. If, however, you do not have a system of measurement and/or have not convinced your sales channel that they must follow up 100% of the inquiries in order to get your average market share, you will continue to waste money and lose to your competitors. But more important, you will suffer anemic revenue and consequently weak profit contributions. Your cost of customer acquisition will simply be greater than it should be.

## Two Business Rules

So far I have described a basic operating rule, the Rule of 45, for managing sales and marketing and for getting the most out of sales leads. If you understand that rule, here are two others that will also help you meet those objectives:

1. 100% Follow-up Rule: Corporations that have a 100% inquiry follow-up policy will sell more than those that don't.
2. 100% Accountability Rule: Corporations that have a 100% accountability policy for lead generation marketing expenditures will spend their investors' money on marketing tactics that can be proven to find buyers.

The combination of 100% follow-up by salespeople and 100% accountability by marketing is the only way to be sure that the company is getting what it is paying for: a predictable return on investment.

## The 100% Follow-up Rule

If you believe in the Follow-up Rule, you will need a policy for managing your salespeople. Here is a sample policy statement that can be used to manage salesperson follow-up:

> Salespeople will follow up 100% of all sales leads and grade each inquiry with a sales resolution code.

This is easier than you think if your sales manager is strong. Admittedly, implementing this into your sales force policy and philosophy is difficult. It takes a stubborn sales manager who will not listen to excuses as to why an inquiry wasn't reached and spoken to. Of course, we know about leads with no phone numbers, those that are geographically undesirable, those on low-priced products, and those from people who inquire but never buy. In spite of all of these excuses, the sales manager's ability to staunchly believe that all prospects are created equal and all deserve to get what they asked for (contact from someone in your company) is the rule that cannot be broken.

The following definition of follow-up will help avoid misunderstanding and provide a common-sense compromise: A salesperson has made at least five conscientious attempts to speak with an inquirer either in person or on the phone but failed. More about this later.

The effort must be made to complete the circle and speak to the person who inquired. How you word this "policy" to your salespeople, and how you enforce it, is up to you. Making it a business rule for the sales department is one way to get the point across.

Once stated, you must have a tool for reporting and enforcement. In the worst of cases you give the salesperson an inquiry by email and ask them to report back. Salespeople will often count on you having too many tasks to bother to follow up with them, so reporting by email for each individual inquiry is haphazard and does little for anyone. It is a constant battle to ask what happened to the inquiries. To solve this you need a process that will allow the salespeople to report with a few clicks and sales management can check, at will, on the results. It must be easy for both sales and marketing to execute.

When the frustration level or the volume of inquiries gets high enough, sales managers start to send inquiries out on spreadsheets and ask that the salesperson complete a disposition for each inquiry. Eventually getting the inquiries back with a disposition on the spreadsheet wears out its welcome because it eats up valuable sales time, and someone in marketing has to transfer all of the information back into some sort of inquiry versus sales comparison program.

Once the company has outgrown the spreadsheet version of accountability, it can follow one of several routes:

1. Use a purchased software product that is just for response management.
2. Use a sales force automation software product that is essentially a contact management program with a calendar, etc., that tracks and reports on campaigns.
3. Use the corporation's CRM program if it has a marketing module for management inquiries. Check on cost to customize and time to complete installation.
4. Go to a customer acquisition management company that provides response management as an Application Service Provider service. Very often these companies offer other services such as fulfillment, inbound telemarketing, and outbound inquiry qualification.

If the company has one of these four options, compliance becomes easier for the salespeople. Depending on the software used, marketing may be able to easily comply with the Accountability Rule and be held answerable for the demand they have created. Compliance by the sales force is in direct proportion to how serious sales management is about the 100% Follow-up Rule and how easy the reporting system is to use.

Many corporate managers want to believe that by spending hundreds of thousands of dollars for CRM software they have solved the issue of inquiry management. Unfortunately, having a CRM (Customer Relationship Management) or SFA (Sales Force Automation) program isn't an automatic solution. Some programs don't have all functions (including the sales campaign management portion) installed. In some cases multimillion dollar "solutions" aren't able to deliver a sales inquiry to a salesperson (much less the resellers). Also, the larger issue is the difficulty of using these programs. The sellers of these programs will insist that "it isn't us" when, after months and years, proper lead distribution still hasn't taken place. But someone is to blame and frankly the salespeople and the prospect don't care about slow installations, etc.; they just want their needs met.

If these programs are not delivering as promised—if a salesperson can't get inquiries from the system in a timely manner—then they should be returned and a refund given. One way around this problem is to give the vendor clear, precise specifications for the program being purchased. In most cases it is just a matter of priorities: Make the management and delivery of a prospect to the salesperson as first priority rather than the last application to be installed.

The definition of follow-up may vary with the product, market, and customer. For instance, the salesperson might need a face-to-face meeting. For some situations this is not possible or economical. The alternative is that they require a salesperson to make as many as five phone calls to reach an inquirer. If the average person were to call 100 people by name within a corporation, they will get through to 25% on the first try, and the same percentages on each attempt. After five calls, they will have reached about 76% of the inquiries. Common sense tells us that there is a diminishing return if a salesperson makes more than 5 calls and never hears back from the inquirer. If the rep has called and left messages and not received a return call, the prospect most likely does not have buying plans. At this point the salesperson can feel justified in closing out the inquiry and giving it a resolution that indicates "could not contact" or "not qualified."

Every sales team will create its own set of rules and methods for complying with the 100% Follow-up Rule. What's most important is that the rule is in place, that there is a system of reporting and measurement, and that the salespeople must comply with this rule as a condition of employment.

Depending on your sales stages, the disposition terminology

you use (sold, bought other, could not contact, etc.), and the system of closing out the inquiry, the final resolution language will depend on the system you have built or bought to give you the reporting you require. (See Chapter 6 for more about resolution codes.)

In order to make the best use of a direct salesperson's time, some companies only follow up on the inquiries that are the most qualified and nurture the rest. This nurture strategy is most often used by companies that produce more inquiries than a typical salesperson can follow up. Nurturing (also called drip irrigation) is the weeding and feeding of an inquiry until that inquiry is "Sales Ready." This can be done through any combination of inside sales, contact center (inside or at a vendor), email, and/or mail. The result is that nothing goes to the representative until the inquirer has agreed that the time is right to talk to a salesperson.

Marketers who have limited control over their channels have challenges of a different sort. They must convince the rep or distributor getting the inquiry that it is in their best interest to not only follow up but also to report on the final resolution. Nevertheless, many companies are doing it today with considerable success. In an article titled "CRM's Missing Link: Acquiring the Customer," Dave Koering, Sales Development Manager for Intermec Corporation (a Seattle-based technology company), said, "The ability to track and refine leads from the inception to an actual sale, and to have that kind of feedback for our marketing group, is one of the biggest positives. And having Web-based access to all the leads that are in the database is important to us."[2]

## How Marketing Complies with the Accountability Rule

The marketing department must put in place the rules and tools that can both measure the salespeople's and the marketing department's compliance. Depending on how your company's products are sold (how much direct control you have over salespeople), you can devise ways for marketing to be held accountable either directly for each lead generating tactic or indirectly through an outreach program of research that touches the inquirers (see Chapter 5).

The goal for the marketing department is to:

1. Spend money (put marketing dollars at risk) only if the return on investment is projected and measurement criteria are decided upon in advance.
2. Identify an ROI goal for every project and dollar spent. The goal for most tactics is an inquiry. How many inquiries can be projected? You can have a raw cost per inquiry, a qualified lead cost, and a closed lead cost.
3. Predict how many sales can be expected as a result of each campaign.
4. Have some measurement of success for programs for which an ROI cannot be projected (branding, some PR, charities, lobbying), recognizing them as strategic investments. If the objective has a dollar value attached, all the better. If not, there should be readership studies, etc., done to have some measurable response.

The marketing policies for reporting on follow-up can be as specific as the one designated for sales. For example:

1. Marketing will be held accountable for 100% of the inquiries it creates and the prospects it distributes to sales.
2. Marketing spending will be adjusted and allocated to marketing tactics that show the greatest return on investment.

The question is, how can the marketing manager be held accountable if he doesn't have authority over the person doing the follow-up? This question is based on the assumption that unless the salesperson complies with the 100% Rule for sales follow-up, the marketing manager can't comply with his (or her) end of the bargain. This is the excuse everyone hides behind: They don't report to me.

But the answer that breaks this circle is simple. The marketing manager reports to the best of her ability from the inquiry system. If the salespeople are not giving the marketing manager complete compliance, the spotlight turns on them, and responsibility is determined accordingly. Thus, the first rule for marketing—that it be held accountable—leads to the second rule, which concerns spending. Marketing managers must spend money on things that work and let their competitors spend money on everything else. This means that the manager needs performance reports in order to make decisions. If the report in Exhibit 2.2 were from your own lead-generation programs, what would you do? Where would you spend your money?

Would you spend more marketing dollars on trade shows or direct mail? The answer at first glance is to pursue the lead-generating tactic that gives you the most sales. Yet we know that one source of inquiries cannot find all of the available buyers in an industry. The step for most marketing managers is to look at the cost for each tactic; if it meets the criteria for a reasonable return on investment, spend more on that tactic or look for other tactics that can give the maximum return. For marketing, it is a constant search for the best fishing hole. If the hole gets fished out, you have to move on.

Marketing is often stymied by conversion rates: trying to figure out how many inquiries and sales can be expected from a particular source. The questions are: If I mail a direct mail piece, what percent will inquire? If I am at a trade show, what percentage of the attendees will come by my booth? And so on. Fortunately, the research can identify the numbers, reflected in industry averages and

---

**EXHIBIT 2.2**

**Sales by Media Source[3]**

| Sold by Source Type | Unit Sales | Sales Dollars | Mkt Budget | Average Cost per Sale | Marketing Percentage |
|---|---|---|---|---|---|
| Online Media | 96 | $ 960,000 | $ 24,000 | $ 250 | 2.5% |
| Media Print | 176 | $ 1,760,000 | $ 45,000 | $ 256 | 2.6% |
| Trade Shows (3 40 x 40 foot booths) | 456 | $ 4,560,000 | $ 120,000 | $ 263 | 2.6% |
| Internet (Website, contact us pages) | 127 | $ 1,270,000 | $ 38,000 | $ 299 | 3.0% |
| Direct Mail (one mailing) | 225 | $ 2,250,000 | $ 67,500 | $ 300 | 3.0% |
| Outbound Lead Gen (1 program) | 45 | $ 450,000 | $ 15,000 | $ 333 | 3.3% |
| Press Releases | 65 | $ 650,000 | $ 32,000 | $ 492 | 4.9% |
| Inbound 800 2 people in-house | 101 | $ 1,010,000 | $ 60,500 | $ 599 | 6.0% |
| Web Seminars (Spring and Fall) | 42 | $ 420,000 | $ 28,000 | $ 667 | 6.7% |
| **Total** | **1333** | **$13,330,000** | **$ 430,000** | **$ 323** | **3.2%** |

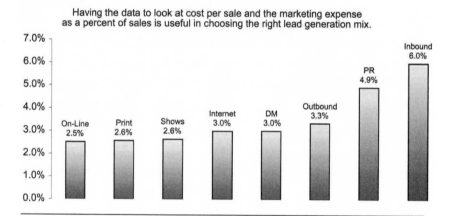

Having the data to look at cost per sale and the marketing expense as a percent of sales is useful in choosing the right lead generation mix.

other, similar kinds of measures, for virtually every inquiry-generating source. Those specific figures change over time as new lead-generating tactics are created, but they are readily available. What is most important is not industry averages for the response you can expect, but the response you can expect for your products in today's marketplace. Recent history can give you that number.

The important idea here is not the Rule of 45, or the time frame, or even the specific follow-up percentage. The important thing is to benchmark for individual products the time frame for closure, the percentage that buy your product, and the current follow-up by the salespeople. Once you know these three bench-marks, you can take action and credit. Taking credit may require you to find ways to report on final results or statistically significant results from surveys. Six ways to prove the return on investment for marketing follow.

## The Six Ways to Prove the ROI for Sales Inquiries

1. **Sales reports: the best way**

   Salespeople report on the disposition of every inquiry through your CRM, SFA/contact management or ASP vendor. If you sell directly to the end user with a direct sales force, you have the control and the management rules to make this happen. The salespeople must realize that if they are to work for you, you must have the final result of every sales inquiry. One simple way is to require that every order placed has a code for the source of the sale. If it is a sales lead, the source must be credited. If the rep can't do it, he cannot place the order.

   In many cases salespeople will report on an inquiry's progress over time, and they will either close it out as dead or give it a disposition code, which shows how it is being worked. We will go over this process in a later chapter.

2. **Compare invoices to inquiries: the most accurate method**

   If you sell direct and you have the names of the people who buy from you, you can compare the name of the company on the invoice (not necessarily the name of an individual) against the original inquiry file. If the sale is made after the initial inquiry, you can claim the connection and credit the source. If the company that bought has inquired several times about the same product, credit the original source.

3. **Did You Buy studies by telephone: a statistically significant way to take snapshots of buying activity for a single product**
   This method is important because someone actually talks to the end user and gets first-hand information. This and the following methods are used to get a statistically valid sample from which you can draw conclusions.

   Measuring the number of people who buy within three months, six months, nine months, and one year (and even longer, if necessary) will reveal patterns you can rely on for forecasting future performance.

4. **Did You Buy studies by mail**
   Similar to Did You Buy studies by telephone, this method is attractive because it can generate the greatest numbers of potential responses at the lowest cost. For every inquiry that comes into the company over an allotted time (e.g., six months), send a self-mailer survey that, once unfolded and refolded, becomes the return vehicle for the survey. Ask the same questions asked in the telephone survey.

   Some companies mail from hundreds to thousands of these surveys a month. Sounds like a lot of money? Not really. The person's name and reference number are printed on the survey form (often when the original inquiry is processed), and the surveys are put aside until the allotted mail date. The postage cost is perhaps the most significant investment. The response you can get on these types of surveys can be from 10% to 25%. For highly specialized fields (e.g., medical devices, with surveys being sent to private physicians), responses rates can be as high as 28%.

   Here's an example of the long-term impact: Let's say that you get 1000 inquiries a month, and six months after the initial inquiry you send this group of 1000 a survey. If you get 15% back for 150 responses and keep a running tabulation of the responses over time, eventually, you will have thousands of completed surveys tied back to the initial inquiries in the database.

The downside to this kind of Did You Buy study is that you will get disproportionate responses from people on the extremes who either love you or hate you. These extremes can slightly throw off the results. Over time, however, when the database of results has thousands of responses tied back to sales for dozens of products over many sources, this type of bias will fade.

5. **Did You Buy studies using email**

This approach is very attractive if people open the email and fill out the survey. Once the button is pushed sending the survey back to you, the results are tabulated and it is easy to take the electronic file and compare it to the inquiry file. The advantages are speed and eliminating the inconvenience and cost of manually processing mailed surveys (data entry of response, etc.). The issue is, can you get people to open the email survey? Proponents of this say they can do it (10–15% average response) with the right subject line. From my experience and given the increasing sophistication of spam filters, I wish them luck.

6. **Comparing warranty cards to inquiries will give you reliable and statistically significant information**

Compare the warranty card information with the inquiry database. If the date of purchase is after the initial inquiry, credit the source with a sale. This is a statistically significant way to prove the ROI for your marketing programs. It is a snapshot in time that builds a case.

We have covered a lot in this chapter. You know how the Rule of 45 can be used to predict the future return on marketing investments, you have follow-up and accountability rules for marketing and sales, and even how to prove the ROI for marketing's efforts.

## Actions to Take from This Chapter

1. Inquiry management must be a formalized process. You require an inquiry management system in order to measure what you are managing. Home grown code, a purchased (most often CRM) or an ASP system provider: regardless of what you chose to manage your inquiries, you must make a choice.

2. Marketing dollars must be accountable. Every marketing dollar spent on lead generation must have the expectation of a return on investment. Strategic investments such as shareholder programs, PR, some branding, etc., should be measured when possible.

3. Sales and Marketing are not immune to process control.

4. Marketing must confirm the follow-up percentage by salespeople (direct or channel) and closing ratios for sales inquiries they have created.

5. The Rule of 45 and its applicability to your product in your marketplace must be benchmarked and confirmed. Only primary research can find the basic numbers you need to predict the future for each of your products. The primary number you are looking for is the percentage of inquiries that will turn into a sale within the average lifetime of a product inquiry. For most, but not all, B2B products this is 45%. For B2C consumer products, the percentage can be higher and the time frame for conversion much shorter.

6. Create two business rules for your marketing and sales departments to ensure that follow-up and accountability are in place.

100% Follow-up Rule: Corporations that have a 100% inquiry follow-up policy will sell more than those that don't.

100% Accountability Rule: Corporations that have a 100% accountability policy for lead generation marketing expenditures will spend their investors' money on marketing tactics that can be proven to find buyers.

7. You must use one of the six ways known to prove the ROI for marketing expenditures:

   a. Sales reports
   b. Compare invoices to sales inquiries
   c. Did You Buy studies by telephone
   d. Did You Buy studies by mail
   e. Did You Buy studies using email
   f. Compare warranty cards to inquiries

# NOTES

1 I first learned about the Rule of 45 from Mike Simon, the president and founder of Inquiry Handling Services. I introduced the Rule of 45 in speeches given at clients' national sales meetings, in articles, and, finally, in the Obermayer, Donath, Crocker, and Dixon book *Managing Sales Leads: How to Turn Every Prospect into a Customer* (Lincolnwood, IL: NTC Books, 1996).

2 CRM Buyer David Koering in "CRM's Missing Link: Acquiring the Customer," *ECT News Network*, July 22, 2004.

3 This is only an example to demonstrate how to compare the cost per sale based on media performance and is in no manner a representative cost for the media shown.

# 3 Sales Inquiries: An Asset with Declining Value

A majority of the dollars invested in marketing go toward some form of lead-generating activity to build a revenue-generating pipeline. These inquiries come into the company in all forms. They trickle in through inbound calls, trade shows, press releases, advertising, direct mail, and the Web. The sources vary, but these names of people and companies with an interest in you have one thing in common: They are an asset because, as described in Chapter 2, approximately 45% will be buying something from someone within one year.

The asset called *sales inquiries* is the most uncomfortable investment the company makes each year because it is the least predictable. While we are encouraged that almost half of the inquirers will buy, we know that buying is tied to a time frame, which means if the inquirer is not followed up, engaged, and sold, that inquirer as a permanent asset to the company will evaporate.

It is a simple but inescapable fact that sales inquiries decline in value month after month. Inquirers have a shelf life, and from the moment they become visible, it is a race to engage and convert suspects into prospects and eventually into buyers at a greater rate than your competitors. Inquiries rot and die if they are not followed up. If you do not identify the potential buyers as quickly as possible, engage, and track every one to the end of their buying cycle, you lose the majority of the money invested in lead-generation activities and subsequent sales, which is the reason you are investing in marketing. It is curious that so many marketers use the term *investing in marketing* and then studiously avoid reporting on the return on the investment.

In an article titled, "Most U.S. Companies Mismanaging New Leads," *Sales and Marketing Strategies and News* reported the findings of an online survey of 800 respondents entitled "Gauging the Cost of What's Lost."[1] The study "suggests that while companies may be good at generating large volumes of leads, more prospects languish because the sales department is too frequently focused only upon closing the most promising and qualified short-term opportunities."[2] The 23-page report found:

- 66.4% of respondents said they would rate new customer acquisition as "very important."
- 43.6% said they are dissatisfied with the way their company goes after new business.
- 72.2% said they believe they could generate over 10% more revenue if business development and prospect-harvesting practices were more effective and 37.34% believe such improvement would convert into more than a 20% increase in revenue.
- 53% believe sales and marketing have a close and collaborative relationship, but only 7% say the two groups work together very effectively to harvest business prospects.
- About 56% convert less than 10% of their prospects into deals; 30% convert less than 5%.
- Most respondents are not satisfied with their conversion rate; only 5% are very satisfied.[3]

So how big a deal—really—is lead management and follow-up? Since leads are the most important creators of wealth in a company, lead management has the broadest strategic as well as tactical implications for any company. It is more than just the loss of a few dollars (or few thousand dollars) spent on a marketing tactic to generate new inquiries. If you prove how many inquiries are not being followed up (by using Did You Buy studies), you will be able to determine the cost of each missed lead by applying your conversion ratio to the number of missed leads as well as the estimated cost of the potential sale. If inquiries are properly managed and accounted for and every inquiry is followed up to its resolution, revenue will increase within 90 to 180 days and, you will have one of several choices to make.

1. **Hire More Salespeople.**
   Expand the sales force and keep marketing spending the same because sales lead follow-up is better. Now all of the potential buyers will be addressed, and many will not be ignored and left to competitors. This is the tactic followed by a software client of mine. Her processes needed tightening and business rules enforced so that no prospect was ignored by a too-busy salesperson. She hired more salespeople.

2. **Spend Less on Marketing.**
   You could spend less on marketing because if salespeople were genuinely maxed out and could not follow up all inquiries, the added lead-generation money was a waste. Marketing as an expense could be reduced.

3. **Spend More on Marketing.**
   Spend more on marketing because the results are more predictable. It makes sense to generate more leads because you are able to profit from them. If you know the pre-

dictable outcome, over time you will sell more than a competitor without a system or the business rules and discipline of follow-up and reporting. Along with the increased spending on marketing will come the inevitable increase in salespeople. Or, in the words of the old saying, "the rich get richer."

# How the 100% Follow-up Rule
# Increases Corporate Profits

The 45% rule and 100% follow-up rule are strategic as well as tactical imperatives for every company. What do these and related business rules do to create wealth in a company? Here is an example:

---

**HOW TO GET SIX CENTS A SHARE MORE BY FOLLOWING UP 100% OF THE INQUIRIES CREATED BY YOUR MARKETING DEPARTMENT.**

**Situation:**
We have a $25 million company in the year just ended.

Marketing stats:
- The average lead cost is $50.
- There are 12,000 leads generated each year. There are 5,400 buyers (45%) in the 12,000 inquiries.
- The company is only following up 3,600 (30% of their inquiries).
- In the 3,600 there are 1,620 buyers.
- They have a market share of 25%.
- They will sell to 405 buyers with an average sales price of $25,000.
- The company spends 4% on marketing each year or $1.2 million, with $600,000 going to lead-generation activities.
- They are forecasted to sell $10,125,000 from leads and their pipeline; service revenue, license fees, and international sales will

contribute to the other $19 million in sales that are needed. This is a nice, neat package.

Financial stats:
- There is a total sales target of $29,125,000 in the coming year.
- The company expects a pretax profit of 11% or $3,203,750.
- The after-tax profit for this year is forecast at 5% or $1,456,250. There are 20,000,000 shares outstanding.
- Earnings per share are projected to be a modest $0.07.

---

But what would happen if inquiry follow-up is 100%? If they follow up on 100% of the inquiries, they will find and identify 5,400 buyers of the 12,000 inquiries rather than just 3,600 (at 30% follow-up). Within those 5,400 buyers a company that has a market share of 25% will find and sell to 1,350 buyers (instead of only 405 sales at 30% follow-up) with an average sales price of $25,000. The sales results from leads will be $33,750,000 vs. $10,125,000

If fixed costs remain the same for this increase in sales as the result of 100% follow-up and the company attains overall sales of $52,750,000, ($33,750,000 + $19,000,000 from other sources), then the pretax profit of the company will be at least $5,802,500 and after-tax profit will be $2,637,500 (5%) or $0.13 per share.

What's six cents more a share? If the company stock is selling at thirty times earnings, at seven cents the stock is worth $2.10 a share, with a book value of $42 million. At thirteen cents the stock is worth $3.90 a share. The evaluation of the company is now $78 million.

Of course we are not taking into account that:

- If fixed costs remain the same except for incremental man-ufacturing and sales expenses, before- and after-tax profits will be much, much greater than what is being shown here.

- If there is a 100% follow-up of inquiries and the marketing manager knows what sources brought in the most sales, he or she will spend more on what works and less on what doesn't. The result will be increased marketing efficiency.
- When the sales department has a 100% follow-up policy and on average twice to three times more prospects are called and visited and quoted, sales will increase in direct proportion to the people spoken to and followed up.
- There will be lower turnover in the sales ranks, which reduces sales expenses as a cost of sales. Sales, marketing, and senior management will sleep better prior to the end of every quarter.

Exhibit 3.1 shows the result of a policy that forces sales to speak with 100% of the people who inquire.

Of course, this is an extreme example, but it is not unrealistic. Follow-up enables a rep to talk to more people, find more buyers, make more sales, increase revenue, increase profits, and increase the value of the company.

## Marketers as Creators of Wealth

The marketing people are the unsung heroes of your company, but their biggest mistake is creating wealth and not taking credit for it. Their programs find millions upon millions of buyers for billions of dollars worth of goods and services. They spend money to find prospects but seldom insist on any proof as to what happened to the prospect. They excuse themselves from reporting on their successes by hiding behind their inability to control the entire process from finding a prospect to closing the sale. As a group, marketing is too polite and courteous; a little rash aggressiveness would do them and their companies some good.

Senior management must cultivate a marketing department

**EXHIBIT 3.1**
**The Product of 100% Follow-up**

| Situation | 30% Inquiry Follow-up | 100% Inquiry Follow-up |
|---|---|---|
| Sales goal for the year (leads + all other sources) | $10,125,000 +$19,000,000 $29,125,000 | $33,750,000 19,000,000 $52,750,000 |
| Pretax (11%) | $3,203,750 | $5,802,500 |
| After Tax (5%) | $1,456,250 | $2,637,500 |
| Earning per share | $0.07 | $0.13 |
| Company book value | $42,000,000 | $78,000,000 |
| Stock at 30 x earnings | $2.10 per share | $3.90 per share |

that has pride in itself and is willing to prove it's own worth with the same aggressiveness as sales. Unfortunately, most marketing managers do not complete the task of creating demand because they think the completion is out of their control. It is in the hands of sales they say. Once those words are uttered and they give up, the excuses never stop coming and their corporations are doomed to continue the cycle of inefficiency and waste of the stockholders money. Salespeople will continue to be inefficient and fail more often than is necessary. Marketing people must work with sales to see inquiries all the way through the customer acquisition cycle and be able to prove their contributions.

The companies that are following this path of finding the greatest number of potential buyers within their servable market have several traits in common:

1. They have a system to manage inquiries.
2. They have business rules to ensure a 100% follow-up of the inquiries.
3. They believe in finding out the resolution of 100% of the inquiries.
4. Marketing and sales management approach customer acquisition in its totality as a team sport.
5. There is a central leader or champion that can motivate and direct both teams.
6. They believe every marketing dollar is precious and should have a measurable, predictable outcome.

And they never forget that sales and marketing is a process. Processes can be measured and improved upon.

## Actions to Take from This Chapter

1. Senior management has to provide the coaching and leadership to ensure marketing and sales work together, shatter the silos of power between these departments, and demand that they operate as a team. They have common goals. Each team will welcome the change.
2. Marketing and sales must report to a believer. A leader.
3. Marketing plans must be tied to sales quotas.
4. Reports must reflect sales and marketing's constant status and improvement. Measure what you manage.
5. Every inquiry must be followed-up and resolved.

### *NOTES*

1 "Survey Report: Most U.S. Companies Mismanaging New Leads," *Sales and Marketing Strategies and News*, November/December 2004, page 9.

[2] 2004 BPM Forum and CMO Council, "Gauging the Cost of What's Lost," co-sponsored by *Sales and Marketing Strategies and News* and *BusinessWeek*, December 2004.

[3] "Survey Report: Most U.S. Companies Mismanging New Leads," *Sales and Marketing Strategies and News*, November/December 2004, page 8.

SECTION TWO **Managing
the Process**

# 4 Defining and Identifying Inquiries, Suspects, Prospects, and Leads

Thus far, I have covered the importance of leads and why properly managed sales leads are the lifeblood of every company. In this and subsequent chapters I will focus on how to get the basics—defining what a lead really is, why you should probe an inquirer about purchase intent, and how an inquiry should be graded or evaluated—right. Getting these basics right is the foundation of the marketing processes already presented and those that will be presented later. You will use all of these processes to properly manage sales inquiries and, consequently, sell more than your competitors. These basics not only make the salesperson more knowledgeable and better able to assess an inquirer's need, but they greatly help the marketing department understand why one inquiry source generates more buyers than another.

## Inquiry vs. Sales Lead

The term *sales lead* has been historically used to describe any inquiry from any source. We hear it used fast and loose:

"I didn't get any good leads last month."

"I didn't make quota because I didn't get any leads."

"Oh, you misunderstood me. I don't need more leads, I need more *qualified* leads."

"Trade show leads aren't real leads; I got those at the show. Marketing doesn't get credit for those!"

"That wasn't a lead you sent me," the salesperson complained. "That was just a name, just an inquiry. That wasn't a *real* lead. You know *anybody* who is going to *buy*—who's *ready to buy*?"

And, of course, everyone is familiar with the role of leads in the movie *Glengarry Glen Ross:*"I need more leads . . . I can't sell anything with these leads . . . Leads are for closers . . . Coffee is for closers. . . ."

The first definition of the difference between a lead and an inquiry comes from the sales rep—the person on the front lines. A lead in a salesperson's mind is someone who has a greater propensity to buy (a true prospect or at least a real suspect) than just an information seeker (an inquirer). When you ask salespeople to describe the difference, you seldom get a clear answer: "I just know one when I see it" is a common response. Probe further and you will get a more definite answer, but that answer will revolve around the degree to which the prospective buyer is ready to buy versus the degree to which he or she is just seeking more information (a tire kicker). Marketing's only refuge in this argument resides with the amount of information that comes along with the inquiry. If there is a lot of information about the buyer's intent, the marketing people feel that they can judge the inquiry and grade it as a qualified lead.

Sales and marketing together can quickly identify good leads. In his book *The Fundamentals of Business-to-Business Sales and*

*Marketing,* John M. Coe says: "Of all the terms in marketing, the one that is by far the most misused and misunderstood is *leads.*"[1]

Dick Evans, the founder of AdTrack, is the first person I have known who stopped calling every inquiry a lead. "An inquiry," he said, " is not a lead. It is a request for information. A lead is an inquiry that has been qualified." A *raw inquiry*, most people will agree, is someone about whom we know very little. It is usually just a name and address and little else to hint at their buying intention. Inquiries most often come from sources that do not let the inquirers tell us about themselves in any depth. This includes print media inquiries, reader service numbers in magazines, PR inquiries from press releases, and virtually any source where the inquirer has not been given a chance to tell you about his or her intent to buy. The truth is that there are many different kinds, levels, or degrees of leads and the inquiries that feed into them.

The best lead reveals itself from information gathered about the inquirer. The more information you have, the more likely you can put inquiries into categories. These categories are based on judgment and can only be arrived at if your marketing department asks questions up-front. The person who inquires wants something from you: information about your products. On a quid pro quo basis (and in the spirit of consultative selling) you should request and get answers to questions. After all, you can't give good answers until you know what the real questions are.

## Profile Questions: Understanding Buyer Intentions and Potential

Companies typically use a variety of media—from hard-copy questionnaires to Internet-based questionnaires to direct contact through telemarketing or other similar follow-up—to get more information about an inquirer's needs and intentions. In more sophisticated companies, when a person inquires about the company's products, the marketer will ask and get answers to "profile" questions 55% to 65% of the time *without* outbound telemarketing. The marketing departments of these companies are on an obsessive hunt to get the most information possible out of every prospect. This means that they will ask questions and leave space for answers in all possible portals of entry into the company.

Without an effort to get answers to profile questions from inquirers, the timid, less sophisticated companies will only get answers to questions for 10% to 15% of the inquiries. This places them at a substantial competitive disadvantage because:

- Marketing cannot place a grade on an inquiry when nothing is known about it. No grade means no ability to judge the initial value of the inquiry source.
- Salespeople will follow up inquiries when they know something about the person's need. The less that salespeople know about an inquirer lead, the less likely they are to pursue it. If they have information about the inquirer, they are much less likely to give up after the first unreturned phone call.

The way to qualify unqualified inquirers (those who did not self-qualify and about whom you know nothing except product interest) is to call them. By using the excuse that you are trying to service the inquirer's specific needs, an outbound caller (call center person) can get the answers to most profile questions. It will take three attempts to complete calling on 60% to 70% of the inquirers (more efficient than the average salesperson), but at this point you have answers to questions on 75% to 80% of the people who inquired. Of course, you can make several more attempts, but those last two calls will reach a point of diminishing returns.

If your lead-generating tactic has given inquirers space to describe their needs (for instance on a business reply card in a direct mail piece, Web contact page, or a trade show lead form) and they tell you something about themselves, salespeople will feel that these people are qualified and deserve to be called leads. So it is easy to see that in order to understand how many leads you have versus inquiries from a particular source, you must get the answers to profile questions.

## Why Profile Questions Are So Important

Salespeople understand the need to uncover answers to questions during the sales call in order to increase their knowledge of customer issues and help them customize a solution that will be bought. Other authors and sales trainers have emphasized question-based selling tactics for at least a generation. Neil Rackham, in *SPIN Selling*,[2] Thomas A. Freese, in *Secrets of Question-Based Selling*,[3] and others say that to be a good salesperson you must ask a lot of questions, listen carefully, create customized solutions, and ask for the sale less often. *SPIN Selling* divides the questions into:

- Situation Questions
- Problem Questions
- Implication Questions
- Need/Payoff Questions

Rackham's approach came from landmark research conducted by his consulting company, Huthwaite, which studied 35,000 sales calls. One of the most significant finds was the answer to a very simple question: In a successful sales call, who does most of the talking? The buyer? The seller? After counting what the two parties said they found that, "In successful sales calls it's the buyer who does most of the talking."[4]

And Freese weighs in with:

> To significantly increase your results, you must be willing to position yourself differently in the sale. This means changing the way you uncover needs, understanding how potential buyers are motivated, using references to create a sense of momentum, and minimizing the risk of rejection to increase your probability of success."[5]

He further adds, "You can significantly reduce your risk of rejection by knowing where the other person stands before you actually pop the question.[6]

*Uncovering needs* are the operative words. You can't uncover a need when you are doing all of the talking or if you aren't asking questions. Rackham insists that situation questions that explore the buyer's present situation are vital. You can't sell without them. [7]

How does this have anything to do with marketing and inquiries? A lot—because a good marketer can ask and put the answers to 8 to 15 questions into a database and pass them to a salesperson. The answers to these questions help the salesperson prioritize a sales call, understand the needs of the inquirer, and avoid asking too many basic situation questions during the first visit. The more the salesperson understands the situation, the faster she can get into the problems she is trying to solve for the prospect. On the other hand, the marketing person needs answers to the questions so that the inquiry source can be judged accurately.

Some marketing people ask if they are being intrusive by asking questions of inquirers. The answer is no: You have been invited to the party; you are not being intrusive. A person inquires about a product, and is happy or at least quite willing to supply the information to the few questions you have every right to ask. Very few business-to-business inquirers or even considered-purchase consumer inquirers are offended by being asked a few questions. You can't know the value of an inquiry unless you know something about the person or company making the inquiry.

Some marketers further ask, "Doesn't it get confusing—asking different questions for all of our products?" The answer is no. Many of the questions you will ask will be common for all products, although some will be application-specific. But conduct an experiment: Ask your salespeople what kinds of information they would like to know about a prospect. Chances are very good that you will have 75% of the questions you'll need to ask—and the majority of those questions will be the same across all product lines. With this in mind you need only ask a few specific application questions by product line.

John Coe contends that the four most accepted questions or parameters that define a lead came from his days at IBM where they used the term BANT[8] (Budget, Authority, Need and Timing).

The kinds of questions salespeople like include:

- Need: product or service?
- Buying time frame for purchase: how soon?
- Number of units?
- Currently installed product?
- Decision-making ability: recommend or specify? A decision-maker?
- Budget?
- Lease or purchase?

Deeper, pain-related questions include:

- Have you had problems with your current product?
- Why do you want to replace it?
- What would your staff most like to see in the new product?

Application-oriented questions can include specific questions that pertain to a specific product's ability to perform. For instance:

- Do you want a three-channel ECG or an eight-channel ECG?
- Plug in or battery operated?
- Fast or slow speed?
- A two-pound laptop computer or a luggable eight-pound PC?

If you know the answers to these questions, you can determine how likely a person is to buy by grading the inquirer. Now, both you and the salesperson have a better idea if the person is just a random inquirer with little or no buying intent versus a potential buyer.

The fact that a person doesn't initially feel like revealing his future plans doesn't mean he isn't a buyer, so you have to ask the questions anyway. The sources of inquiries that encourage the inquirers to reveal something about themselves are:

- The Web "contact us" page
- Inbound toll-free calls
- Toll calls
- Business reply cards (BRC) in direct mail pieces
- Trade show inquiries
- Coupons in advertisements (with room for 2 or 3 short questions)
- Business reply cards in advertisements (tip-in or blown-in)
- Post card decks (tight, but possible)

Each of these lead sources has the space to ask for and encourage the inquirers to tell you something about themselves. This is obviously easier in B2B than in B2C as B2C inquirers (consumers) may want to hide information. B2Bers will give up information about their company if you ask questions in a nonthreatening manner. Unfortunately, both B2B and B2C inquirers have a common trait: They lie. They will only tell you the information they feel is necessary to get what they want from you. For 20% to 40% of the inquirers, not revealing their complete buying plans is common. After all, most of these people are professional buyers (not in purchasing but in every other department).

Other inquiry sources, such as traditional print media and press releases, create inquiries (most often through readers service numbers), but unless the person is driven to the Web or calls your toll-free number, you may only get their product interest, name, address, and phone number. These are inquiries (not leads) because you don't know anything about buying intent. They may be hot or cold or somewhere in between, but unless someone talks to them, they and their value are unknown. The grade level for these inquirers is a low letter grade (D) or the term *cold*. In most companies these are sent to the salespeople as raw inquiries.

Because so little is known about them, salespeople tend to treat them with disdain versus the inquiries that had a high grade and included the answers to profile questions. I have personally experienced that if these low-grade inquiries are followed up at the same rate as those with a high grade, the buying percentage between them will not be significantly different. (Of course, I am excluding those bogus leads that are actually students and competitors.) But that's what puts salespeople off—the bogus leads—even if it is to their own detriment. When they get a few competitors and students, salespeople begin to paint the entire group of inquiries with the same negative brush and, as a result, ignore real buyers.

## Grading the Inquirer

Once you have the answers to profile questions, you must grade the inquirer. Grading is crucial because it enables marketing to judge the inquirer and the source of the inquiry. It helps salespersons identify the "hottest" inquiries and thus prioritize their time efficiently. Grading is the result of a combination of answers from the profile questions. If the person says he or she will buy in three months, has the budget, and is the decision-maker, this is a "hot" or an "A"-grade-level inquirer. If, however, the person is not a decision-maker, says he will not buy for nine months, and doesn't have a budget, the suspect will be considered cold or a "D"-level inquirer.

Grading is necessary because you want to know the potential of the inquiry as soon as possible. You can best do that by making an informed evaluation when it *first* enters the database. For example, when you return from a trade show, you enter the inquiries into your system. This is the first level of measurement, which will be the first pass of grading. At this point they are "suspects." Some inquiries will be considered A, some B, and so forth, in as many descending grades as you use. Regardless of how the inquirer/suspect progresses through the system until they "buy or die" (buy or not buy during the selling cycle), they should always carry the brand of the original grade. Only then will you able to measure the result of the source or even the source type (print ads, PR, direct mail, shows, banner ads, Web, outbound lead generation, webinars, etc.). If you grade the majority of the inquiries, you will be able to answer questions such as:

1. Which inquiry source gives our company the most A- and B-level inquirers?
2. Which inquiry source gives us the most C- and D-level inquirers?
3. Which source *type* (advertisements versus direct mail versus shows versus the Web) gives us the most A and B inquirers?

The questions and answers can be startling for those who want to stop making marketing decisions by intuition and start generating sales leads based on performance. The end result will be apparent when you are able run reports showing the performance of specific sources of inquiries and source types by grade and sales contribution.

## Creating Questions and Answers and Coding the Results

When you create the inquiry questions, code the responses with numbers for each category so you can easily organize the answers in a database. Having the same code number for the same question across all product lines allows you to compare answers for the question. For instance, isn't it nice to know what percentage of people buy in three, six, or nine months for Product A versus Product B?

At this point, assume you are asking and getting the answers to profile questions. You now can choose how to grade them. If you are using an inquiry management vendor, you most likely will use Boolean Logic, which looks at the answers to specific questions and derives a grade from those answers. For instance, a Boolean question may be:

> If the inquirer answers yes to question 1A (buy in three months) and yes to question 2B (is budgeted) and yes to 3B (makes final decision), the inquiry is a grade A or "Hot."

With Boolean Logic, you are not using a point system for the answers to each question. Your logic is simply, "If this, then that." You are not limited by the number of "If this, then that" instructions. Boolean Logic is a more elegant solution to grading and in many respects simpler to use if it fits your software system.

The alternative to Boolean Logic is to use a grading system that attaches points to the answers for each question that are rolled up into a grade that translates into a designation of Hot, Warm, Cool, Cold or A, B, C, D. While not as exquisite as Boolean Logic, such a system can work very well.

Let's look at some typical questions and how they are graded.

1. How soon will you be making a purchasing decision?
   A. 0–3 months          (30 points)
   B. 4–6 months          (25 points)
   C. 7–9 months          (15 points)
   D. 10–12 months        (10 points)
   E. 13 months or longer (5 points)

Note that the shorter the time frame, the greater the point value.

2. How much storage do you require?
   A. 51–250 GB           (10 points)
   B. 251–375 GB          (20 points)
   C. 375–500 GB          (30 points)
   D. 501–750 GB          (40 points)

In this instance we give more points to the larger storage opportunity than the time frame for purchase (40 vs. 30). A good salesperson can move the time for purchase up, but he or she cannot usually change the size of the opportunity.

3. Your title:
   A. On the committee     (3 points)
   B. Recommends           (5 points)
   C. Specifies            (10 points)
   D. Decision-maker       (15 points)

In the example for question 3, a decision-maker will get a higher point value than someone who is on a committee or recommends, but the total points available are lower than for time or storage. Questions for installed products, pain caused by the current problem, etc., may not have points at all. Generally 5 to 6 questions contribute to a score when you are using a numbers or Boolean system.

If the same question is asked in the exact same way for all products regardless of source type (ads, direct mail, shows, Web, PR, toll-free calls, outbound calls, etc.) or specific source (XYZ Trade Show, June Direct Mail Campaign, October Insertion in X Magazine), you will be able to compare answers to this vital question and see if it varies by source or source type.

Comparing this information by specific source will show a vast difference between ads and direct mail, shows versus Web inquiries, etc.

Grading is crucial to your system because it will drive the marketing step that finally delivers a qualified inquiry to the salespeople. Many companies will not pass an inquiry to their salespeople unless the inquirer is Hot or Warm (or an A or B). If the inquirer is not in one of these categories, the inquirer is nurtured by marketing (mail, email, telemarketing) until it is either developed into an A or B or killed off as a prospect lacking potential.

Ignore the contents of this chapter at your peril. You must define what a lead is—as an organizational asset, not an abstract intellectual exercise. And you must ask those questions that will help both sales and marketing determine the potential value of the inquiry and develop the process that will give you the kind of information that both sales and marketing agree is needed. What will naturally follow is the distribution of inquiries and leads to your sales channel.

There is a vast difference of opinion about what should be

given to the salespeople for follow-up. While I agree that the salesperson's time should be protected from chasing unqualified inquiries, a little voice in my ear reminds me to be cautious about being too aggressive and overzealous in screening (nurturing) inquiries to the point that true buyers are virtually given (by default) to competitors. While 20% to 25% of sales inquiries can (and should) be screened out because they are students or competitors or prisoners looking for mail from home, the rest will have some degree of "warmth" and should be passed along to the salespeople.

I contend that it is the salesperson's job to turn weak and only moderately interested or qualified buyers into true buyers; this is what they do for a living, not just grabbing the low-hanging fruit. Of the 75% or so inquiries left after initial screening, it is only the real salesperson who can do the final screening and pursue the 45% within the 75% left.

## Actions to Take from This Chapter

1. Everyone in the organization, especially marketing, must understand the difference between a sales lead and an inquiry. An inquiry is the name of the person or company that is unqualified (you know little about them). A lead is an inquiry that is qualified so that you have an idea about the buyer's intent.

2. Go to the salespeople and ask them, "What are the four to five qualifying questions you want asked of an inquirer before you speak with them? The answers will be the basis for your profile questions. You must use profile questions in every communication where it is possible to ask the question and record the answer. These include:

   • Trade shows inquiry forms
   • Contact pages on your Web site

- Business reply cards in your direct mail campaigns
- Inbound toll-free calling scripts

3. For the inquiries that do not give you answers to profile questions, call them prior to passing the inquiry to your sales channel.

4. Create a grading system for the inquiries and make sure the answers are visible in reports and on the lead sent to the sales channel.

5. When you ask questions, record the answers in the database, and grade the inquirers, you will have to decide whether to nurture the unqualified, delete the unqualified, or pass them along to your salespeople. The decision to pass or delete can only be based on your product, the average sales cycle, the value of the sale, etc. Generally the higher the value of the sale the more likely you will pass all inquirers, regardless of whether or not they reach a qualified status, on to the salesperson (obviously screening out students and competitors).

## NOTES

1 John M. Coe, *The Fundamentals of Business-to-Business Sales and Marketing* (New York: McGraw-Hill, 2004), page 113.

2 Neil Rackham, *SPIN Selling*, (New York: McGraw-Hill, 1989).

3 Thomas A. Freese, *Secrets of Question-Based Selling* (Naperville, IL: Source Books, Inc., 2000).

4 Neil Rackham, *SPIN Selling*, (New York: McGraw-Hill, 1989), page 9.

5 Thomas A. Freese, *Secrets of Question-Based Selling* (Naperville, IL: Source Books, Inc., 2000), page 1.

6 Ibid, page 14.

7 Neil Rackham, *SPIN Selling*, (New York: McGraw-Hill, 1989), page 10.

8 John M. Coe, *The Fundamentals of Business-to-Business Sales and Marketing* (New York: McGraw-Hill, 2004), page 126.

# 5 Speaking in Numbers

---

The salesman was on the spot with his sales manager. He wasn't making quota and no one was happy. The Director of Marketing was asked to sit in on the meeting because the core of the unhappy salesperson's argument was, "I'm not getting any leads."

The Director of Marketing had his reports with him and didn't think the sales rep was going to win this one. The rep had been consistently given inquiries, but there was little information coming back from the rep. The conversation continued:

"Look, Mike," the Sales Manager said into the speaker phone. "You're not making quota, so what are we going to do about it?"

"But I haven't been getting any leads," Mike pleaded. "After all, I am supposed to get some help from Marketing, and it just isn't happening."

Ray, the Sales Manager, turned to the Director of Marketing and asked, "Tom, what's your side of it?"

Tom said, "The reports show that Mike has been getting an average of 21 new product inquiries a month for the last 6 months. Except for one or two sales he hasn't told us anything about the 128 inquiries we've given him."

"Those weren't leads," Mike interrupted. "Nobody wanted to buy anything!"

Trying to refrain from showing his frustration, Tom said, "Mike, we gave you 40 inquiries from trade shows, 20 from inbound calls, 35 from advertising, 25 from the Web, and another 8 from PR. I can't see how you can say you didn't get any leads."

"Well, that's just it," Mike replied, "Those weren't leads. The show leads were from local shows I attended. You didn't give me those. The advertising leads were trash, and nobody returned calls. The Web leads, I think, were mostly from competitors. And what you call PR leads were from students and low-level guys who can't make a decision. And if there isn't a phone number, it isn't a lead as far as I am concerned. Besides, a good third of the names were on the far northern end of my territory. I never get up there. And then what about the duplicates? I bet there were at least ten duplicates in the group. Those aren't leads. I got maybe five decent leads out of the whole bunch." Thinking he had sufficiently answered everyone's objections, Mike fell silent.

"Mike," the Marketing Director responded, "we paid for those exhibits, and we asked you to send the inquiries to us. The advertising leads aren't trash. Look at the titles for the people. A third said they have an immediate need. I can't control it if people inquire from areas you don't want to drive to. And as for the duplicates, I can see that there are six names on this report we'd consider to be duplicates. It isn't unusual that someone will inquire on the Web and also call in, and that appears to be what happened. For two of the names, the products they inquired about are different. We don't count those as dupes. Maybe the others inquired a second time because you didn't reach them. Of the 128 inquiries given to you, 22 are considered 'Hot—qualified.' You have one of the lowest reporting percentages in the sales force. With an average cost of $118 per inquiry, we've spent $15,000-plus on lead generation in your area in the last six months, and none of us have anything to show for it."

"As for telling us what happened to your leads," the Marketing Director pressed onward, "the other salespeople have reported on 60% to 75% of what we've given them. From their closing percentages, you should have turned at least 11 sales so far from the inquiries given to you. What happened?"

The conversation didn't get any better from that point.

I never heard what happened with this salesperson, but through the years I have talked to dozens just like him. When they make this many excuses, the outcome isn't good. The salesperson was trying to save his job by blaming Marketing for not doing theirs. But the marketing director had the numbers at his fingertips. He knew the salesperson had not reported on inquiry disposition. He knew what percentage of the inquiries was considered qualified, the average disposition by others in the sales force, and even the typical closing ratios. If he hadn't run off the reports before he joined the meeting, the salesperson might have put enough doubt in the sales manager's mind to think that the problem was Marketing.

When sales are down and the finger pointing starts, marketing management had better be able to fall back on the numbers. Have the sales reps reported on inquiry disposition? Have they followed up on qualified leads? What percentage of the inquiries has been considered qualified? What has the prior average disposition by the sales force been? What are typical and realistic closing ratios? The director of marketing who isn't able to respond to these kinds of questions with hard numbers—the language of management—finds himself on the losing side of a stalemate with sales reps and will appear to be spending the company's money unwisely.

## Process Control in Sales and Marketing

Every product we buy today will be obsolete in the near future. It will be improved. It will do its work faster, it will look better, it will last longer, it will be smaller or bigger. "It" is always the outcome of someone's desire to improve. Yet the area that is not improving and changing at the same speed as our products and the manufacturing processes that make them are our sales and marketing processes. With the exception of the Internet, these areas and channels have remained relatively immune to change.

We've heard it all before: Marketing management claims that branding, exhibits, direct mail, public relations—in essence, the entire mix of tools used by Marketing—can't be measured on their contribution to sales. Nevertheless, sales and marketing can be measured and controlled to the extent to which you make the effort. For the marketing and sales managers who want to measure what they manage and constantly improve and grow and be more successful than their competitors, the numbers—in charts and graphs and spreadsheets—are readily available and useful.

What it gets down to is when you don't want to do something, one excuse is as good as another. The ultimate judge, therefore, of who is measured and upon what, should be in the hands of the managers who have a responsibility for finance, sales, and marketing. Finance always has an interest because ultimately it is the shareholders' money that is being wasted on marketing budgets that go unmeasured and unaccounted for by the group that spends the money (Marketing) and the group that most benefits from the results, Sales.

## ROI Reporting: The Proof

The term *ROI* is bandied about by many marketing managers, but ask them what they mean, and they'll give you a business school definition. Ask how that definition applies to the money entrusted to them and most hem and haw in search of an answer. Jack Keenan, President of Deciding Factor, once said that, "Most people use the term 'ROI' to stand as a calculation to show the value of something, but it's also a code word for 'business justification.'"[1]

If we accept the thought that we must business-justify everything we do, somehow the hunt for justification is easier because we can divide justification into areas that make the most sense to us and our discipline. With business justification you have hard and soft returns on investment. Soft returns are most likely the raw numbers that indicate that we are winning or gaining, but these measurements do not always lead to a hard business-justification result. For instance, you can look at a brand aware-ness study and find out that more people are aware of your prod-uct today than they were six months ago. You can look at readership awareness studies of advertising and decide whether or not you have reached your goals of getting your advertisement read. But none of these measurements of the marketplace actually tells you what you have sold as a result of your marketing dollars. For this you need either primary research that talks to everyone who has inquired or reports from your salespeople through your response management system, sales force automation system, campaign-tracking system, or CRM systems that give you the results.

How you decide to measure is a direct result of the tools you have available to use, your own ambition to show a return, and the company's ability to pay for the programming necessary to extract the numbers. The bottom line is the ultimate measure-ment: marketing closure for every inquiry generated from every lead source.

Management must understand that some items in marketing are not measurable for a dollar return, and others are very meas-urable down to the penny. Some managers will try to be judged on total revenue generated from a campaign: We spent $20,000 and got $80,000 in return. In his book *Marketing ROI*, James D. Lenskold insists that the only way to measure a genuine return is to look at the percentage return on investment.[2] He insists on taking the total revenue (less the cost of goods and the cost of promotion and other sales expenses) and dividing the resulting gross profit by the cost of the lead generating. The result is a percentage return that allows you to say, "For every dollar we spend we get $1.20 in return."

This supposes, of course, that you can find out the resolution of an inquiry. For a company with a direct sales force where the end-user resolution is easily attainable, full closure can be fairly easy. For those who have indirect channels of selling, coming to a complete resolution of every inquiry is probably not economically or physically possible. You probably will have to be content with methods that give you statistically significant reports by which you can guide your marketing spending.

## Benchmark Where You Are Now

Regardless of your channel of distribution, you have to be able to know where you currently stand on sales-lead closure before you can decide which actions you must take to improve the system and increase the percentage of inquiries you close. To begin, you must benchmark current follow-up and sales-lead closure and then move into the improvement phase. Improvements are on both sides of the aisle—sales and marketing—and those will be covered later in Chapter 16.

To start, go to the marketplace and find out the most recent benchmark numbers. You want to know:

1. **Percentage of Sales Lead Follow-up:**
   The current percentage of follow-up by the salespeople/channel. I am not referring to the *reported* follow-up by the salespeople, but the *actual* follow-up reported by the end users. Is follow-up at 10% or 90%? Once you know exactly where it is, you can begin to plan accordingly to improve it.

   • Look up follow-up on your SFA, CRM, or the response management vendor.

- Go to the prospects (end users) to find out if a salesperson has contacted them. This is covered in the Did You Buy section that immediately follows.

2. **The Percentage of People Who Have Bought at Specific Intervals of Time.**
   While I have said that the Rule of 45 shows that 10% to 15% of B2B inquirers buy within three months, 26% buy in six months, and 45% within one year, this can vary. You should find your own time benchmark for each product in your line. In B2C the conversion rates may be much greater. I prefer to use three-month intervals to determine the conversion rates over time, but if you have a consumer product, you might find that you are wise to measure sales conversion rates on a monthly basis.

3. **What They Bought.**
   This may be different from what they inquired about.

4. **Who Is Still in the Marketplace?**
   You want to know at every point of measurement exactly what percent of the universe is still in the marketplace.

5. **What Percentages Are Buying from Your Competitors?**
   Once you know who has bought, you need to know the percentages that buy from your competitor versus you.

6. **The Reasons They Are Buying.**
   You must know why people are buying either your product or the competitive product. Keep open-ended text to a minimum.

7. **The Percentage That Wants to Hear from You.**
   You need to know what this number is. If the salesperson or reseller has not called on the prospects, their opinion of your ability to sell and service their needs declines over time. For many years I have seen the number of people

who still want to see a company rep after six months to be as high as 50% and after one year still at 15%.

One of the best ways to get this information is by going to the people who initially inquired. These are called Did You Buy studies and there are several ways to do the study.

## Did You Buy (DUB) Studies

I love Did You Buy (DUB) studies because of their impartiality and because they can be replicated and the results compared; decisions can be made from each study or from a combination of studies. These studies are good for products regardless of value or typical time frame for closure. If the DUB is properly done, the results are difficult to argue with, and actions can be taken to improve the follow-up and closure of sales inquiries.

A DUB study should have the following:

1. **A minimum of 100 completed questionnaires.**
   Two or three hundred is even better as it will reduce your error rate.

2. **A single common source: a specific magazine insert, a specific trade show, a specific direct marketing piece, etc.**
   Don't mix sources. Different sources should have different studies. Don't mix inquiries from several trade shows, even if the show attendees have the same titles or even if the show is in the same city.

3. **The inquiries must be from the same point in time.**
   Don't mix the inquiries from three different insertions from succeeding quarters of a print media campaign. The inquiries should be from a fairly specific point in time

(exactly 3, 6, 9, or 12 months since the inquiry was generated)—of course, plus or minus 30 days.

4. **From a single product.**
   Do not mix in different products or even the same product with different values.

Calls to the inquirer work better than snail-mailed or email surveys. Calls tend to get a broader and better representation of your audience. The one exception is if you have a mailed Did You Buy study that goes to all inquirers at a specific trigger date, say, six months. The volume and consistency make up for any biases.

The first Did You Buy study should use four of the same-sized groups of inquiries, one for each time frame (3, 6, 9, and 12 months). Follow the routine—same products, same source, and at least 100 completed questionnaires—for each time period. These four surveys will enable you to benchmark your product in the marketplace and establish your market share numbers. You will know the conversion ratios at each timed benchmark (i.e., each three-month increment), and—what's more important—you will know the conversion ratios of competitors and your own follow-up or lack of it.

The same approach can be used to track a single group of inquirers over a one-year period. The group's performance can be measured at 3 months and revisited at 6 months to determine those that have not bought; the same can be done at 9 and 12 months intervals. At this point you have some numbers that talk to you, and more importantly they talk to everyone in the organization. A typical study will find out:

- The percentage of inquiry follow-up by your salespeople.
- The percentage that purchased someone's products.
- The percentage that purchased your products.
- The reasons why they purchased the product.

- The percentage that is still in the marketplace at each benchmark in time.
- Whether they want to hear from you.

DUBs go to the person who inquired and ask them what action they have taken in addition to the actions taken by the company. The questions asked (without marketing getting too carried away) have to be short and multiple choice. You are after hard numbers that can be projected and compared by product from source to source and time period to time period. The purpose of these studies is to continually show what happens to inquiries from different sources so that decisions can be made to replicate what works and avoid what doesn't work. Salespeople telling you after the fact what happened to the inquiry is great, but hearing first-hand from the prospect is even more important. Eventually, it is always the combination of the results from multiple sources over time that gives marketing and sales the information it needs to improve the process.

Typical DUB questions are:

1. Did you get the information you needed (printed collateral or electronic files) and that you requested?
   ___ Yes ___ No

2. Has a salesperson representing this product contacted you?
   ___ Yes ___ No

3. Have you purchased a product yet?
   ___ Yes ___ No

4. If yes, who did you buy from?
   (List most common companies)

5. Why did you buy?
___ Price
___ Delivery
___ Features
___ Location
___ Currently have other products from the company
___ Enter whatever you need to know but don't over do it.

6. If you have not purchased, are you still in the market?
___ Yes ___ No
If yes, when: ___ 30 days ___ 90 days ___ 180 days

7. Would you like to hear from a salesperson?
___ Yes ___ No

# The Methods Used for DUB Studies

There are probably more than the three ways listed here to perform DUB studies, but these approaches will give you what you need at a reasonable price. Each—mail, telephone, online—has its advantages.

## DUB by Mail

Trying to perform DUB studies by mail takes time, patience, and money. To begin, you make your database choice (a single-product inquirer from a single point in time from a single source). Because you need at least 100 questionnaires filled out and returned, you may have to mail as many as 500 to 1,000 questionnaires to get the minimum of 100 for a valid study. **Time to completion is generally five to six weeks.**

Enclose an incentive—a one dollar or even a two dollar bill—in the mailer to induce recipients to spend their time filling out the questionnaire. Some people suggest using five dollars or even ten dollars can get the desired result. Anything over two dollars is

overkill. First of all, the money is more a sign of respect, of grati-
tude, than actual market-value-based compensation. After all, if
someone's time is worth more than one dollar, it's probably also
worth more than five dollars. And, actually, if it isn't worth more
than that, they probably can't afford your product.

Also, the issue here is that everyone in the mailing will have to
get the incentive, so the cost could be considerable. Instead of giving everyone money, you can enter all inquirers in a drawing.
This option is a mixed blessing because you might have legal fees
to ensure that the drawing is legal in all the states where the inquirers reside. However, it can cut your incentive budget by two-
thirds by giving away a special electronic gismo worth $500
versus putting $5 in each envelope for 1,000 people.

Your checklist for a DUB study is short:

- List (500 to 1,000 names. Same product, same place in
  time, same source.)
- Incentive (helps but is not 100% necessary)
- Printing and mailing cost
- Tabulating and report writing cost

The issue with mailed DUB studies is that you could get bi-
ased results. People who love your company or product or, the reverse, hate the company or the product, can skew the results. For
instance, if you like the car you are driving and get a questionnaire in the mail from your car company, will you be more likely
to fill out the questionnaire and return it? Probably. The same is
true if you really dislike it. Mailed DUB studies can get some
thoughtful responses because the recipient will take the time to
fill it out in his or her own words, not just to check the boxes but
thoughtfully fill in the comments or pen text areas.

The big downside for mailed DUB studies is cost: You are
paying for something that as many as 95% of recipients won't

complete (if you're lucky 5% to 20% will fill out the question-naire) and for the time it takes to mail and get the results. If you create the mailer and send it out (a few weeks at best) and wait for the response (another three weeks for 90% of the response) and then go through tabulation and report writing, you have about five to eight weeks tied up in getting results. Not very efficient.

## Email DUB Studies

An increasingly common method of conducting the DUB is an email survey that uses the same questions used in a mail survey. They are placed in an email message or made available via a link that connects to the questionnaire. Participants are often drawn to complete the questionnaire because of an incentive (e.g., a drawing for an iPod, etc.). The biggest advantage of email DUB studies is time. Results can be tabulated and reported in hours. When time is a factor, email surveys can deliver. **Time to comple-tion is one to two weeks, most of which is devoted to report writing.**

The downside of email DUB studies is that the response rate or percentage drops dramatically, so it may take several times as many names to get the same minimum 100 completed question-naires that you would get by snail mail. Email response is not what it used to be.

## Telephone DUB Studies

I like telephone DUB studies because you can get the most unbi-ased results from the fewest number of names. You can work a relatively small list and call the people on the list several times until you get a live person on the phone and a completed ques-tionnaire. Sometimes incentives are used but not as much as with mailed or online surveys. **Time to completion can be two to three weeks, depending on how many completed surveys you want. It** can take as many as three calls to a group of 200 to 225 names to eventually speak to 100 people willing to take the 3 to 5 minutes a phone-based DUB interview will still take.

## Lead Management Reports You Can Use

Without reports, you don't know whether most of the efforts of sales and marketing are making a contribution or are just a waste of time and money. Reports reflect the ability of marketing to find buyers and for sales to close the inquiries.

Mark Friedman, President of the Velos Group, an inquiry management consulting company, recently said to me, "I don't know any companies with unlimited marketing budgets, so it is critical that they are able to objectively measure which programs are working to drive revenue and profits and which ones aren't. The only way to do this is to develop the infrastructure to measure ROI for each marketing program and allocate limited budgets to those programs that demonstrably support the company's sales and profit objectives. Once done, the value of the enterprise increases dramatically as companies generate more consistent and predictable revenue flows."[3]

The infrastructure is a system to manage the inquiries and reports to tell you where you have been so that you know where to spend money on future marketing campaigns.

What follows are several reports that marketing and sales departments can use to determine whether or not their sales and marketing processes are in or out of control. The primary information in these reports can most likely be cross-indexed in many ways. For instance, want to look at what was sold by you or a competitor by source, source type, rank, and sales dollars? It's easy to do with most reporting systems today. The key is knowing what to ask for. Make your own list of reports to get what you need most.

Month-end reports allow you to view the performance of lead-generating sources, source types, products, and inquiries sent to the sales channel by office, region, or representative on a regular, logical basis, though ad hoc reports pulled off the system on demand also have value. Many software packages provide a suite of decision-making reports and most of the better inquiry management vendors allow access to most of the data on their systems online.

The reports I am showing here are divided into three sections:

1. Month-end reports showing the previous 12 months by representative, source, source types, product sales closure, and follow-up by sales region.
2. Return on investment reports showing the percentage of return for a dollar invested, sales by source, source types, original rank, and inquiries by rank.
3. Typical profile question results showing time frame, budget, how to buy, role, needs, and application.

As you view software packages and vendors, make sure your report needs are known *prior* to signing the purchase order. Before the system goes live, make sure the basic reports are in place. Survey all users to see what they will need to make better decisions.

You don't need all of the reports shown in the samples given here, but you will probably find at least five to six that will address your needs. These sample reports are created by me, but similar to reports from my previous book on inquiry management as well as my experience as a consultant and an employee of the two pioneer companies for inquiry management: Inquiry Handling Service and AdTrack Corporation.

## Total inquiries by representative and region, by month, for prior 12 months (Exhibit 5.1)

This is a very important report for both sales management and marketing. Being able to see how many inquiries a region and representatives are getting on average and comparing this to the quotas and sales results is vital. Is someone exceeding quota? How many inquiries and qualified leads are they getting? Are they getting these on the same products that they are selling? If you give them more, will they sell more? The reverse is true for the salesperson not making quota. Note the reported follow-up percentage. See Exhibit 5.1.

## Campaign Report: Inquiries by Source, by month, for prior 12 months (Exhibit 5.2)

Inquiries in this report are counted and identified by specific source. It could be a *specific* advertisement in a newspaper or magazine on a particular day (or month), *a specific mailing piece* in a direct mail campaign, a specific trade show, etc. For the sake of brevity, the sample in Exhibit 5.2 does not break out every ad insertion, although in actual practice it should. The report shows the event of the inquiry flow by months. Identifying the inquiries by source is crucial to later showing the sales resolution of the in- quiries from that source. Look at the bar chart and the inquiry count for each month in the exhibit. Do inquiries trend upward to support sales? Is the count large enough each month?

## Inquiries by Source Type (media), by month, for prior 12 months (Exhibit 5.3)

Inquiries by Source Type (or event or media) shows the contribu- tion of these types to the inquiry mix. The typical source types are:

## EXHIBIT 5.1
## Inquiries by Rep and Region by Month for Prior 12 Months

Inquiry Results by Region by Representative

| | Follow-up % | Jan | Feb | Mar | April | May | June | July | Aug | Sept | Oct | Nov | Dec | Total |
|---|---|---|---|---|---|---|---|---|---|---|---|---|---|---|
| Eastern Region | 68% | 84 | 48 | 58 | 64 | 72 | 116 | 94 | 121 | 108 | 113 | 120 | 118 | 1116 |
| M. McIntosh | 64% | 23 | 6 | 13 | 21 | 18 | 22 | 18 | 19 | 21 | 25 | 34 | 25 | 245 |
| B. Habereder | 45% | 26 | 16 | 9 | 10 | 11 | 28 | 22 | 36 | 22 | 27 | 29 | 13 | 249 |
| W. Turner | 81% | 22 | 11 | 14 | 16 | 27 | 32 | 36 | 34 | 38 | 29 | 26 | 35 | 320 |
| D.Evans | 89% | | | | 17 | 16 | 34 | 18 | 32 | 27 | 32 | 31 | 45 | 252 |
| P. McClure | 15% | 13 | 15 | 22 | | | | | | | | | | 50 |
| | | | | | | | | | | | | | | |
| Southern | 43% | 73 | 41 | 31 | 56 | 57 | 79 | 79 | 87 | 117 | 115 | 122 | 89 | 946 |
| G. Holcomb | 45% | 16 | 3 | 4 | 10 | 13 | 18 | 23 | 21 | 38 | 27 | 33 | 28 | 234 |
| M. Freidman | 65% | 21 | 8 | 6 | 21 | 22 | 11 | 21 | 23 | 33 | 39 | 44 | 22 | 271 |
| C. McCaslin | 33% | 25 | 22 | 9 | 13 | 14 | 22 | 23 | 22 | 28 | 32 | 26 | 18 | 254 |
| S. Newcomb | 75% | 11 | 8 | 12 | 12 | 8 | 28 | 12 | 21 | 18 | 17 | 19 | 21 | 187 |
| | | | | | | | | | | | | | | |
| South Central | 76% | 50 | 44 | 46 | 86 | 68 | 53 | 48 | 80 | 63 | 67 | 76 | 66 | 747 |
| R. Kean | 78% | 15 | 11 | 9 | 6 | 18 | 15 | 6 | 13 | 10 | 12 | 16 | 12 | 143 |
| R. Hagle | 82% | 0 | 0 | 0 | 0 | 16 | 12 | 8 | 22 | 18 | 15 | 14 | 15 | 120 |
| C. Evans | 79% | 17 | 18 | 18 | 44 | 22 | 11 | 22 | 23 | 21 | 22 | 24 | 18 | 260 |
| P. Wasley | 82% | 3 | 3 | 2 | 18 | 12 | 15 | 12 | 22 | 14 | 18 | 22 | 21 | 162 |
| S.Campanale | 77% | 15 | 12 | 17 | 18 | | | | | | | | | 62 |
| | | | | | | | | | | | | | | |
| Mid-West | 44% | 81 | 46 | 35 | 50 | 79 | 52 | 73 | 66 | 56 | 53 | 54 | 56 | 701 |
| C. Evans | 55% | 21 | 15 | 6 | 18 | 21 | 17 | 15 | 19 | 18 | 15 | 18 | 28 | 211 |
| P. Nasser | 65% | 23 | 15 | 7 | 6 | 18 | 12 | | | | | | | 81 |
| B. Lindsten | 32% | 3 | 12 | 13 | 9 | 19 | 11 | 26 | 19 | 17 | 16 | 18 | 13 | 176 |
| D. Lyding | 77% | 34 | 4 | 9 | 17 | 21 | 12 | 32 | 28 | 21 | 22 | 18 | 15 | 233 |
| | | | | | | | | | | | | | | |
| Western Region | 82% | 111 | 40 | 60 | 57 | 80 | 86 | 75 | 103 | 68 | 67 | 76 | 67 | 1128 |
| M. Burkett | 89% | 34 | 12 | 13 | 17 | 22 | 32 | 12 | 19 | 21 | 17 | 19 | 11 | 315 |
| D. Mayers | 82% | 32 | 17 | 15 | 13 | 21 | 17 | 10 | 23 | 15 | 11 | 15 | 16 | 256 |
| J. Sprouls | 83% | 22 | 5 | 14 | 11 | 19 | 18 | 21 | 19 | 14 | 18 | 17 | 22 | 248 |
| C. Dixon | 75% | 23 | 6 | 18 | 16 | 18 | 19 | 32 | 42 | 18 | 21 | 25 | 18 | 309 |
| | | | | | | | | | | | | | | |
| Total | 64% | 399 | 219 | 230 | 313 | 356 | 386 | 369 | 457 | 412 | 415 | 448 | 396 | 4638 |

- Advertising: Print, which includes magazines, newspapers, even newsletters. This report may show a total number for all inquiries from print media, but it will most often show the detailed breakdown of every print media event that contributed to the total number.
- Advertising: Online for Web advertising, including pay per click.
- Advertising: radio

# EXHIBIT 5.2
## Campaign Report: Inquiries by Sources by Month, for Prior 12 Months

**Campaign Inquiries by Source**

| | Jan | Feb | Mar | Apr | May | June | July | Aug | Sept | Oct | Nov | Dec | Total |
|---|---|---|---|---|---|---|---|---|---|---|---|---|---|
| Biotech today | 132 | 125 | 113 | 156 | 143 | 133 | 145 | 133 | 139 | 163 | 167 | 175 | 1724 |
| Clinical Chemistry | 102 | 57 | 87 | 67 | 78 | 56 | 58 | 75 | 122 | 113 | 136 | 126 | 1077 |
| ClinChem Today | 52 | 44 | 65 | 87 | 54 | 65 | | | 53 | 65 | 84 | 88 | 657 |
| SEO on CCL Product PFC | | | | | | | 32 | 45 | 46 | 56 | 66 | 42 | 287 |
| AACC Show | | | | | | | | | 265 | | | | 265 |
| Pittsburg Conference | | 225 | | | | | | | | | | | 225 |
| Local Shows | | | 52 | 64 | | 45 | | 44 | | 67 | 44 | 65 | 381 |
| Z02 Analyzer New Prod. PR | 135 | 115 | 22 | 15 | 5 | 2 | | | | | | | 294 |
| Quick Release New Prod. PR | | | | | | 238 | 122 | 4 | 8 | 7 | | | 379 |
| Double Quick Test PR | | | | | | | | | | | 55 | 185 | 240 |
| Google Clin Chem Ad | 156 | 145 | 154 | 187 | 156 | 148 | 147 | 167 | 187 | 125 | 135 | 112 | 1819 |
| Spring Direct Mail - Hosp. | | | | | 134 | 76 | 10 | | | | | | 220 |
| Fall Direct Mail Hosp. | | | | | | | | | 15 | 195 | 75 | 45 | 330 |
| Internet Contact Form | 114 | 125 | 234 | 246 | 245 | 175 | 155 | 175 | 185 | 211 | 123 | 125 | 2113 |
| Web Seminar Spring | | | 185 | | | | | | | | | | 185 |
| Web Semianr Summer | | | | | | | 167 | 89 | | | | | 256 |
| Web Seminar Fall | | | | | | | | | | | 135 | | 135 |
| Telemarketing Campaign | | | | | 115 | 105 | 122 | 169 | | | 125 | 54 | 690 |
| Toll-free 800 calls | 81 | 88 | 66 | 52 | 55 | 42 | 65 | 69 | 156 | 145 | 105 | 99 | 1023 |
| Totals | 772 | 924 | 978 | 874 | 985 | 1085 | 1023 | 970 | 1176 | 1147 | 1250 | 1116 | 12300 |

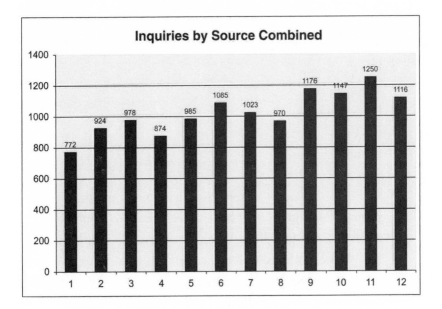

**Inquiries by Source Combined**

---

**EXHIBIT 5.3**
**Inquiries by Source Type (Media), by Month, for Prior 12 Months**

Inquiries by Source Type

| | Jan | Feb | Mar | Apr | May | June | July | Aug | Sept | Oct | Nov | Dec | Total |
|---|---|---|---|---|---|---|---|---|---|---|---|---|---|
| Advertising Print | 209 | 199 | 164 | 190 | 177 | 144 | 109 | 145 | 225 | 320 | 365 | 414 | 2661 |
| Advertising Online | 65 | 54 | 65 | 54 | 44 | 54 | 56 | 67 | 54 | 75 | 86 | 76 | 750 |
| Direct Mail | 85 | 245 | 45 | 174 | 112 | 23 | 225 | 126 | 26 | 175 | 110 | 25 | 1371 |
| Inbound 800 | 41 | 58 | 54 | 52 | 55 | 42 | 40 | 30 | 156 | 75 | 35 | 25 | 663 |
| Internet SEO | 212 | 245 | 234 | 335 | 345 | 313 | 212 | 245 | 347 | 285 | 285 | 186 | 3244 |
| Outbound Lead Gen | | | | | 115 | 105 | 122 | 225 | | | | | 826 |
| PR | 120 | 75 | 45 | 30 | 140 | 85 | 75 | 105 | 132 | 78 | 110 | 114 | 1109 |
| Exhibits | 50 | 50 | 250 | 34 | 50 | 18 | 50 | | 257 | 50 | 75 | | 884 |
| Web Seminars | | 134 | | 105 | | 145 | | 184 | | 165 | 124 | | 857 |
| Total | 782 | 1060 | 857 | 974 | 1038 | 929 | 889 | 1127 | 1197 | 1223 | 1315 | 974 | 12365 |

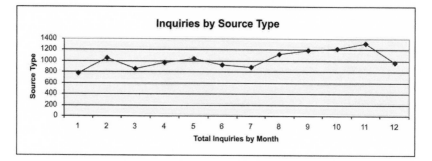

- Advertising: television
- Press releases
- Trade shows
- Direct Mail
- DRTV
- Seminars: live
- Seminars: online
- Web Home Pages: Often there is some confusion because some other source may have driven them to your Web site. Excludes pay for click, which is reported by source type.
- Telephone (toll-free and toll calls): These calls are driven by other inquiry sources, yet many companies will track them as their own source. When they end up in this source category, it is often because the caller does not remember what has driven them to call.

**EXHIBIT 5.4**

**12-Month Inquiry Summary by Source Type**

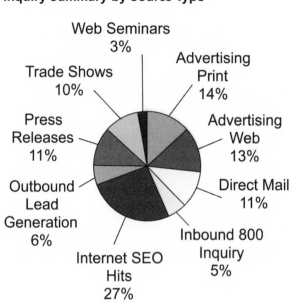

Web Seminars 3%
Advertising Print 14%
Trade Shows 10%
Press Releases 11%
Advertising Web 13%
Outbound Lead Generation 6%
Direct Mail 11%
Internet SEO Hits 27%
Inbound 800 Inquiry 5%

In this report we show a second chart and a pie chart to demonstrate the month to month flow of inquiries. You have to ask yourself:

1. Is the flow constant month to month?
2. Does the volume of inquiries support sales in that quarter?
3. Do inquiries generally trend upward over time to reflect the increasing need to see more product sold from month to month?

## 12-Month Inquiry Summary by Source Type (Exhibit 5.4)

This pie chart gives you an exact count of inquiries by source and how each source contributes to the lead generation effort for a

12-month period. Running this report month to month for each source type (Web, shows, direct mail, etc.) gives you a feeling for mix. If sales dip, you can look back three to four months before each dip to see if the mix of inquiries or the volume has changed.

## Inquiries by Product, All Campaigns by month, for prior 12 months (Exhibit 5.5)

This is considered to be one of the more crucial reports. It shows how many inquiries have been generated by product, month by month, over the trailing 12-month period.

When you view this report you must ask yourself:

1. Has inquiry generation for this product been consistent month to month over the 12-month period? Have there been blackouts (no inquiries for a few months) or brownouts (a dip in inquiries for a few months)?
2. Are the inquiry numbers sufficient to match quota requirements? Simply stated, have you generated enough inquiries to support the quota goals of the company? See Exhibit 5.5.

## Inquiry Sales Closure Reports (Exhibit 5.6)

Whether you call it inquiry closure, or sales lead resolution, every company will have categories for the close out of inquiries and leads. Showing this by region and sales representative is very telling. Compare the closure rates with sales performance by representative and regional manager. This report shows the results of a salesperson "closing the loop." Depending on the sales resolution categories you have created, the inquiry or lead must eventually be closed out and assigned to one of the categories.

Judging a sales inquiry involves not so much steps as resolution(s) of the inquiry: What happened when the salesperson called on the inquirer? The most common resolutions are:

- Sold: Just for you, not for a competitor. Dollars are listed (or lifetime value).
- Bought competition: List dollars (or lifetime value) and competitor.
- Sales pending.
- Future prospect: This is a parking spot for an inquirer. The salesperson will re-contact the prospect. Marketing will probably help in future re-contact programs.

---

**EXHIBIT 5.5**
**Inquiries by Product, All Campaigns by Month, for Prior 12 Months**

Inquiries by Product -12 Months

| | Jan | Feb | Mar | April | May | June | July | Aug | Sept | Oct | Nov | Dec | Total |
|---|---|---|---|---|---|---|---|---|---|---|---|---|---|
| Back-up Assemblies | 14 | 15 | 17 | 35 | 12 | 5 | 12 | 21 | 26 | 13 | 10 | 12 | 192 |
| Bearings | 32 | 34 | 45 | 43 | 23 | 22 | 12 | 15 | 35 | 55 | 42 | 35 | 393 |
| Guide Lock Assemblies | 12 | 16 | 16 | 17 | 25 | 33 | 22 | 12 | 56 | 34 | 22 | 33 | 298 |
| Piston Rings | 12 | 22 | 8 | 15 | 12 | 17 | 15 | 19 | 14 | 14 | 33 | 28 | 209 |
| Rod Wipers | 11 | 2 | | | | 10 | 25 | 12 | 3 | 22 | 20 | 18 | 120 |
| Rod Sets | 32 | 45 | 62 | 45 | 54 | 48 | 43 | 47 | 63 | 76 | 66 | 34 | 615 |
| Structural Components | 14 | 23 | 2 | 5 | | 16 | 3 | 4 | 12 | 34 | 15 | 10 | 138 |
| Telescopic Sets | 10 | 11 | 10 | 15 | 15 | 18 | 15 | 14 | 22 | 28 | 40 | 20 | 218 |
| Thrust Washers | 14 | 22 | 12 | 18 | 22 | 3 | 5 | 32 | 3 | 16 | 19 | 15 | 178 |
| U-Cups | 25 | 32 | 45 | 43 | 34 | 44 | 33 | 36 | 45 | 49 | 52 | 33 | 471 |
| Vee Rings | 12 | 13 | 15 | 18 | 15 | 22 | 14 | 18 | 22 | 32 | 40 | 35 | 256 |
| Totals | 188 | 235 | 232 | 254 | 212 | 235 | 199 | 230 | 298 | 373 | 359 | 273 | 3088 |

Inquiries by Product—12 months

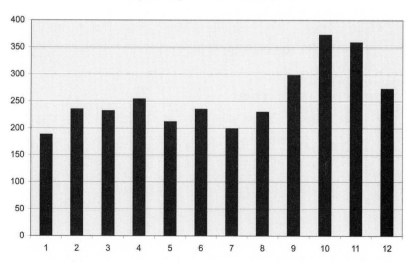

(Continued)

**EXHIBIT 5.5 (Continued)**
**Inquiries by Product, All Campaigns by Month,**
**for Prior 12 Months**

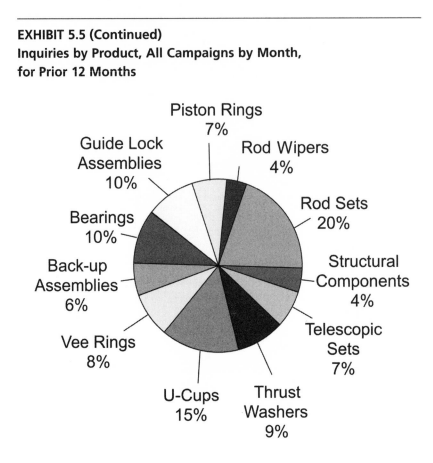

- No contact: This usually means that after three to five phone calls the inquirer is unreachable.
- Information only: This is the place to put students, competitors, prisoners, etc.
- Not qualified: They may not have a need for your specific product, you may have an overfeatured product, or it could be the company can't buy your particular product.
- Not interested: Very often these are inquirers who, for various reasons, have no interest. They could have been looking for a different product, spent the money on another product, etc.

## Inquiries by Region, Follow-up (Exhibit 5.7)

Similar to Exhibit 5.6, this shows inquiries sent and followed up. Very plain and to the point, those that are not reporting on the inquiry resolution stand out in this report. Is the Northwest with only a 36% reported follow-up also lagging in quota attainment? Is the South with 88% reported follow-up making quota (and making it more consistently) than others? Is the Southwest, with the largest number of inquiries, even with only a 70% follow-up, making more sales than anyone else? After all, the total inquiries followed up for this region are more than the total number of inquiries received by the other regions.

## Return on Investment (Exhibit 5.8)

This report shows the dollar and percentage return on a dollar invested. It looks at the source type of inquiries and shows sales in dollars and units. The cost of goods is shown as an estimate for sales expenses, the gross margin, the promotional cost, and the return on investment in dollars and percentage return on investment. This report follows the thoughts and writing of James D. Lenskold and his basic ROI approach in his book, *Marketing ROI*.[4] This sample does not take into account net present value, discount rates, etc. If you want to measure every dollar spent on marketing, buy his book. See Exhibit 5.8.

## Sold vs. Lost to Competitors by Source (Exhibit 5.9)

Sold vs. Lost to Competitors gives you invaluable information. It will indicate market share by company (requires further breakdown by competitor). If you see sales increasing for competitors, you know you have a problem. Pulling these reports monthly or at least quarterly shows you who you are gaining on and who is gaining on you.

How accurate are these reports? This simple bar chart shows

## EXHIBIT 5.6
## Inquiry Sales Closure Reports

| | Sold | Bought Competitor | Sales Pending | Future Prospect | No Contact | Information Only | Not Qualfied | No Interest | Past 12 Months | % of Total |
|---|---|---|---|---|---|---|---|---|---|---|
| Eastern Region | 87 | 77 | 10 | 95 | 248 | 148 | 94 | 181 | 940 | 29% |
| S. McNealy | 15 | 16 | 3 | 31 | 43 | 22 | 18 | 39 | 187 | |
| J. Robert | 25 | 27 | 2 | 21 | 82 | 28 | 22 | 36 | 243 | |
| S. Johnson | 25 | 16 | 3 | 26 | 38 | 32 | 36 | 74 | 250 | |
| F. Hager | 22 | 18 | 2 | 17 | 85 | 66 | 18 | 32 | 260 | |
| Southern | 53 | 41 | 31 | 46 | 170 | 79 | 103 | 121 | 644 | 20% |
| L.A. Harbor | 12 | 3 | 4 | 10 | 34 | 18 | 23 | 43 | 147 | |
| S.W. Smith | 16 | 8 | 6 | 21 | 76 | 11 | 45 | 35 | 218 | |
| B.J. Jobs | 14 | 22 | 9 | 13 | 38 | 22 | 23 | 22 | 163 | |
| M. Newcomb | 11 | 8 | 12 | 2 | 22 | 28 | 12 | 21 | 116 | |
| South Central | 104 | 26 | 35 | 63 | 72 | 40 | 48 | 76 | 464 | 14% |
| C. Gerst | 38 | 6 | 7 | 16 | 17 | 12 | 6 | 18 | 120 | |
| S. Bean | 41 | 9 | 8 | 18 | 33 | 9 | 8 | 27 | 153 | |
| C. Evans | 22 | 8 | 18 | 10 | 10 | 8 | 22 | 13 | 111 | |
| C. Smith | 3 | 3 | 2 | 19 | 12 | 11 | 12 | 18 | 80 | |
| Mid-West | 96 | 22 | 24 | 60 | 144 | 52 | 76 | 177 | 651 | 20% |
| L. Skolowski | 36 | 5 | 6 | 18 | 32 | 17 | 15 | 19 | 148 | |
| D. Farabow | 23 | 12 | 7 | 6 | 34 | 12 | 3 | 82 | 179 | |
| B. Lindsten | 3 | 1 | 2 | 9 | 22 | 11 | 26 | 33 | 107 | |
| D. Liting | 34 | 4 | 9 | 27 | 56 | 12 | 32 | 43 | 217 | |
| Western Region | 98 | 40 | 12 | 66 | 79 | 69 | 75 | 90 | 529 | 16% |
| M. Burkett | 21 | 12 | 3 | 32 | 15 | 22 | 12 | 23 | 140 | |
| M. Roth | 32 | 17 | 5 | 13 | 25 | 17 | 10 | 33 | 152 | |
| S. Tai | 22 | 5 | 4 | 16 | 18 | 17 | 21 | 12 | 115 | |
| D. Mayers | 23 | 6 | 0 | 5 | 21 | 13 | 32 | 22 | 122 | |
| Total | 438 | 206 | 112 | 330 | 713 | 388 | 396 | 645 | 3228 | 100% |
| Percentage of Total | 14% | 6.4% | 3.5% | 10.2% | 22.1% | 12.0% | 12.3% | 20.0% | | |

the sources of inquiries and product in units sold and lost to competitors. If the competitors' sales have been tracked by name, you can drill down further to see which source is bringing in the most sales for you and your individual competitors. Whether you are getting the information from everyone in sales or even getting information on the older inquiries (those over five to six months old) is an issue. This type of report, however, becomes more accurate over time because as the reports grow the error rate will drop as hundreds and then thousands of sales are reported. The numbers won't lie in the long run. See Exhibit 5.9.

**EXHIBIT 5.7**
**Inquiries by Region—Follow-up**

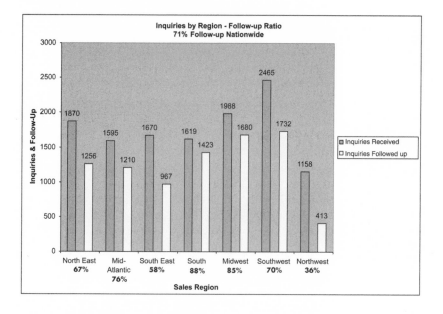

## *Sold by Media Campaign—Sale by Source (Exhibit 5.10)*

A report showing sales by source gives the exact source of the inquiry: a specific exhibit, PR release, print advertisement, DRTV spot, live seminar, online seminar, or direct mail campaign. This report doesn't attempt to get into a percentage return. It just looks at the sales in units and dollars versus the lead generation budget and shows a percentage of the dollars spent on the budget. See Exhibit 5.10.

## *Sold by Source Type (Exhibit 5.11)*

Sold by Source Type allows you to compare sales by media category. You should be able to see all sales from public relations, direct mail, print media, seminars, television, etc., as categories. A pie chart can be used to show sales and the percentage of each

**EXHIBIT 5.8**

## Return on Investment

| Sold by Source Type | Sales | Revenue | Cost of Goods | Sales Expense | Gross Margin | Promotional Cost | Total Return | ROI |
|---|---|---|---|---|---|---|---|---|
| Direct Mail | 35 | $ 350,000 | $ 175,000 | $ 70,000 | $ 105,000 | $ 65,000 | $ 40,000 | 62% |
| Exhibits | 36 | $ 360,000 | $ 180,000 | $ 72,000 | $ 108,000 | $ 55,000 | $ 53,000 | 96% |
| Inbound 800 Inquiry | 22 | $ 220,000 | $ 110,000 | $ 44,000 | $ 66,000 | $ 35,000 | $ 31,000 | 89% |
| Internet | 45 | $ 450,000 | $ 225,000 | $ 90,000 | $ 135,000 | $ 45,000 | $ 90,000 | 200% |
| Outbound Lead Generation | 45 | $ 450,000 | $ 225,000 | $ 90,000 | $ 135,000 | $ 38,000 | $ 97,000 | 255% |
| Paid Media Online | 46 | $ 460,000 | $ 230,000 | $ 92,000 | $ 138,000 | $ 44,000 | $ 94,000 | 214% |
| Paid Media Print | 43 | $ 430,000 | $ 215,000 | $ 86,000 | $ 129,000 | $ 95,000 | $ 34,000 | 36% |
| Press Release | 16 | $ 160,000 | $ 80,000 | $ 32,000 | $ 48,000 | $ 35,000 | $ 13,000 | 37% |
| Web Seminars | 34 | $ 340,000 | $ 170,000 | $ 68,000 | $ 102,000 | $ 36,000 | $ 66,000 | 183% |
| **Total** | **322** | **$ 3,220,000** | **$ 1,610,000** | **644,000** | **966,000** | **448,000** | **$ 518,000** | **116%** |

**EXHIBIT 5.9**
**Sold vs. Lost to Competitors by Source**

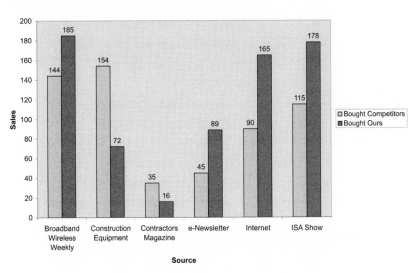

media's contributions. In a spreadsheet with the total cost for the media and the sales, it will show the sales multiplied by media. The more detailed the information you have, the better decisions you can make. This chart is in unit sales, but it could just as easily be sales dollars (in average sales or lifetime value). See Exhibit 5.11.

## *Sold by Original Rank (Exhibit 5.12)*

I love seeing the granularity of sales made by the original rank of the inquiry. How many sales came from inquiries ranked as "A" or "Hot" inquiries versus those that were labeled "B" or 'Warm."

I had a client (a seller of software) who did not believe in the value of trade show inquiries. To the president and his sales managers the only inquiries worthy of follow-up were the names of those people who downloaded a trial copy of their software. And they were right about the value of the inquirer who downloaded

**EXHIBIT 5.10**
**Sold by Media Campaign (Sale by Source)**

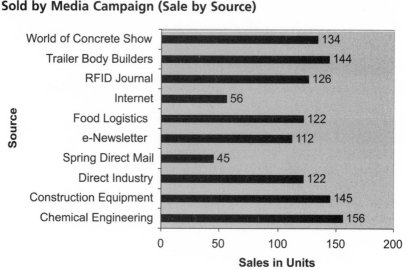

the trial product, but they found out that they were dead wrong about trade show inquiries. The first step was a Did You Buy study of trade show inquiries, which showed that the company was losing to competitors for trade show inquiries at a much higher rate than other inquiries. The next step was to stop swiping badges without taking profile information and to begin ranking the show inquiries. They found an inordinate number of hot leads. Many of them, to everyone's surprise, bought the products without a 30-day trail. Trade show exhibit inquiries became a serous source of hot leads and sales for the company.

## Inquiries by Rank, 12-Month Total (Exhibit 5.13)

When inquiries are ranked, either with a letter, number, or temperature, it is vital to know what percentage of the inquiries are A or Hot, etc. If a company has loose criteria for grading inquiries and calls too many of them hot when they're not, salespeople lose confidence in all inquiries (and the marketing department that

**EXHIBIT 5.11**
**Sold by Source Type**

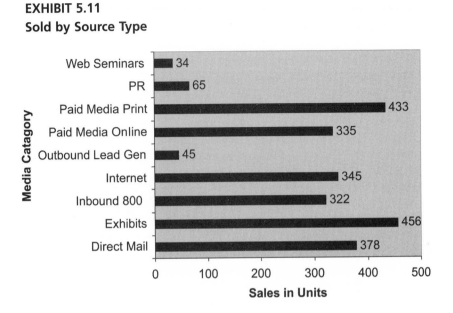

**EXHIBIT 5.12**
**Sold by Original Rank**

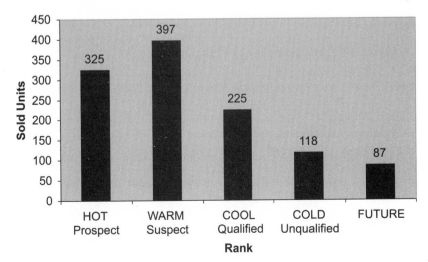

**EXHIBIT 5.13**
**Inquiries by Rank, 12-Month Total**

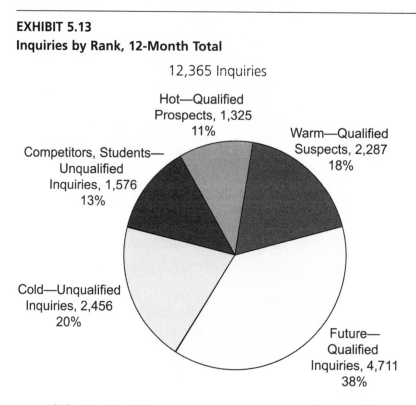

12,365 Inquiries

Hot—Qualified Prospects, 1,325 11%

Warm—Qualified Suspects, 2,287 18%

Competitors, Students— Unqualified Inquiries, 1,576 13%

Cold—Unqualified Inquiries, 2,456 20%

Future— Qualified Inquiries, 4,711 38%

created the inquiry). As a company gets more sophisticated, it will know the number and percentage of hot and warm inquiries it needs to make quota. See Exhibit 5.13.

## Profile Questions and the Reports

What follows are five typical "profile" questions and the reports that are the result of tabulating all of the answers. As you know by now, profile questions are used to help salespeople understand a need before they call on a suspect. The answers to each question, when combined with the answers to other profile questions, allow you to "grade" an inquiry so you know it's value (and the value of the source) when it enters the company. For instance, running reports that show you the source of the inquirers for

**EXHIBIT 5.14**
**Need for Product: Timing**

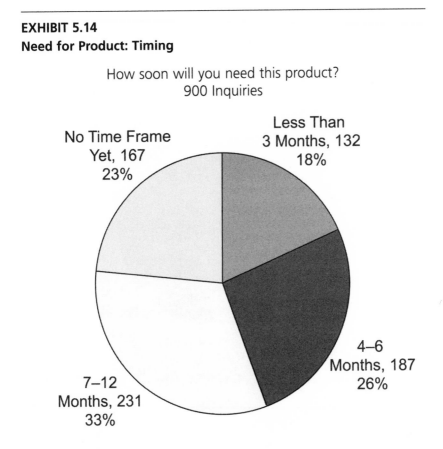

How soon will you need this product?
900 Inquiries

No Time Frame
Yet, 167
23%

Less Than
3 Months, 132
18%

4–6
Months, 187
26%

7–12
Months, 231
33%

decision-makers or the source of those that buy in a shorter period of time is valuable.

## Profile Question: How soon will you need this product? (Exhibit 5.14)

Every salesperson wants to know the time frame for a potential purchase. Some sales trainers argue that this question should not be asked too soon. Personally, I like asking it because I like knowing the time frame on average for inquiries. Once I know this, I can also look at the time frame answer by source, source type, and product. See Exhibit 5.14.

**EXHIBIT 5.15**
**Budgeted for Purchase**

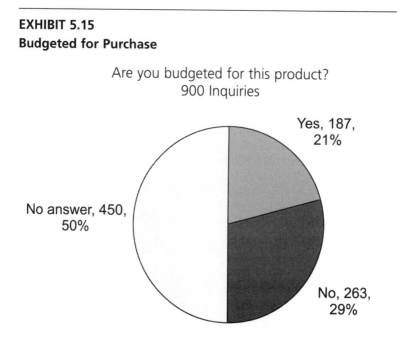

Are you budgeted for this product?
900 Inquiries

Yes, 187, 21%

No answer, 450, 50%

No, 263, 29%

## *Profile Question: Are you budgeted? (Exhibit 5.15)*

This isn't being asked as much as it once was, but you'll still see it. It isn't unusual to see suspects pass over this question. But for those who answer it, it is great to know. Running this information against source, source type, and product is invaluable.

## *Profile Question: How will you acquire this product? (Exhibit 5.16)*

Not everyone wants or needs to ask this question. If it isn't applicable, replace it with another situation or pain-related question that the salesperson needs to know. If you don't know what this might be, ask your salespeople.

## *Profile Question: What is your role in evaluating this product? (Exhibit 5.17)*

This question falls into the pushy category and not everyone will answer it. It isn't unusual to have many people inquiring from the

**EXHIBIT 5.16**
**Method of Product Acquisition**

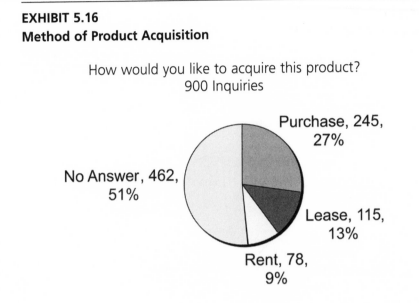

How would you like to acquire this product?
900 Inquiries

Purchase, 245, 27%

No Answer, 462, 51%

Lease, 115, 13%

Rent, 78, 9%

**EXHIBIT 5.17**
**Role in Product Evaluation**

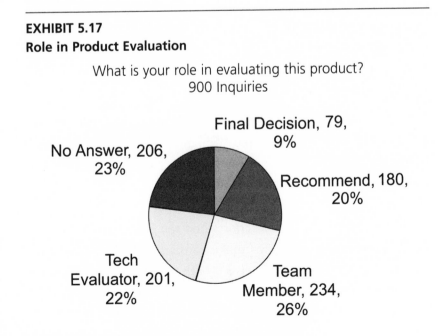

What is your role in evaluating this product?
900 Inquiries

Final Decision, 79, 9%

No Answer, 206, 23%

Recommend, 180, 20%

Tech Evaluator, 201, 22%

Team Member, 234, 26%

---

**EXHIBIT 5.18.**
**Product Application**

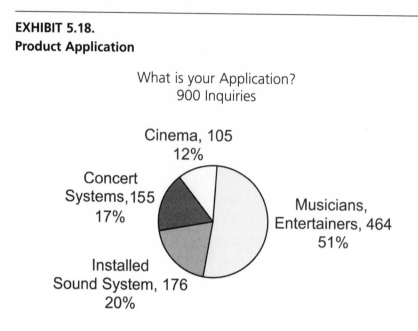

What is your Application?
900 Inquiries

Cinema, 105
12%

Concert
Systems, 155
17%

Musicians,
Entertainers, 464
51%

Installed
Sound System, 176
20%

same company on the same product and knowing their roles is important. Cross-tabulating this question by source, source type, and product is interesting.

## Profile Question: What is your application? (Exhibit 5.18)

This question gets to the nature of the inquiry. How the product will be used is crucial to some companies. A disk storage company may ask about gigabits of storage, a medical device company may ask where the product will be used (office, hospital, or ambulance).

I have found that these reports and the information that can be found several layers down make you wiser and more competitive in the marketplace. Twelve-month reports show blackouts and brownouts. You can look at trends and see that demand always drops before sales failures.

## Actions to Take from This Chapter

1. Determine where you are on sales lead follow-up and closure. Do Did You Buy studies to benchmark your current status. Don't be afraid. Just think how good you're going to appear in three months when you have fixed the problem.

2. Determine the reports you will need to control and adjust the sales and marketing process. No, you don't need 15 to 20 reports to manage the system and the people in sales and marketing.

## *NOTES*

[1] Jack Keenan, President, Deciding Factor, *CFO Magazine*, September 1999.

[2] James D. Lenskold, *Marketing ROI: The Path to Campaign, Customer and Corporate Profitability*, (New York: McGraw-Hill, 2003).

[3] Mark Friedman, Velos Group, Tustin, Calif., www.velosgroup.com.

[4] James D. Lenskold, *Marketing ROI: The Path to Campaign, Customer and Corporate Profitability*, (New York: McGraw-Hill, 2003), page 19.

# 6 Managing Inquiries

It isn't easy to do, or the ability to do it wouldn't be a competitive advantage!

"Do we have an inquiry management system? " the president asked his chief marketing officer. "No? We need one. Go get a system and let me know how it's working."

Or if the company has a CRM system, the CMO (Chief Marketing Officer) is liable to say, "Well, we have a CRM system to manage the inquiries, but marketing can't seem to get the reports it needs . . . and the salespeople don't like it . . . so they use it as little as possible."

The makers of all of them—CRM systems, SFA systems, contact management systems—promise to solve the problems of inquiry management. Unfortunately, senior management often views response management and everything that goes into it as a minor software/labor function. To an extent they are right: The labor for data entry, fulfillment, territory management, and lead distribution can be performed by lower-cost administrative staff and secretaries. However, the problem is that few of these managers understand that lead management is vital to a company's operational health and that this vital function shouldn't be relegated to people's "other duties as assigned"—i.e., do it when they have time. The potential for waste is enormous: Millions can be spent on lead generation and defending advertising that will generate no revenue. While many in sales and marketing management understand that sales cycles can be long, few understand that inquiry management is a time-vital function and that the life cycle for leads is short if a competitor beats you in the door.

Senior management usually can't believe that after all the money being spent on CRM the inquirers still go without receiving the information they requested (literature or PDF files), a call from a salesperson, and a final resolution of the inquiry. Unfortunately, this is a prime example of management once again confusing a desired end result with the purchase of software.

Deciding how to solve this issue isn't as easy as someone saying, "Buy software." Fixing the inquiry-management problem is only difficult because it crosses department boundaries. Traditionally, inquiry management has usually defaulted to marketing because marketing creates demand and then processes the results. A typical sales manager wants someone to get the fulfillment done and get the leads and not worry about anything else. The *anything else* is reporting and accountability, and maybe that's all it was when Mike Simon, the president and founder of Inquiry Handling Services, pioneered this business niche in 1966. Mike sold the accountability of marketing and sales as benefits of managing leads. The snail mail used for sending leads to salespeople and getting them back to find out which advertisements or direct mail piece or show found buyers was cumbersome. Filling out lead-inquiry forms and sending them back for record updating wasn't popular among salespeople.

All of that changed in 1994, with the advent of the popularized Internet. Inquiries are now sent via email or posted on the Web behind password-protected sites. Now, reporting on the disposition of an inquiry requires a few clicks; everything is easier and more convenient. With the disappearance of paper or faxed "leads," the irritation of sending inquiries back and forth through mail or by fax is gone.

I estimate that 90% of U.S. companies in B2B manage sales inquiries in-house with the remainder managed at service companies that specialize in response management. Information about B2C is obscure, but I suspect the percentage is similar to B2B. With the advent of sales force automation (SFA) and customer relationship management (CRM) software, many companies that formerly outsourced these services are tempted to manage inquiries in-house. More recently, with the increase in application service provider (ASP) software, the trend toward the total in-house management of inquiries has accelerated. The problem of managing inquiries hasn't been solved as much as it has been assumed to have been solved . . . because managers have collectively spent untold millions on software.

But results have not matched the promise. Managers, tempted to think that purchased software has solved the problem, ignore the time-consuming, cross-department labor that goes into managing inquiries. When a company forecasts the cost for software and labor, they don't realize that the larger issues are cross-department tension, a lack of cooperation, and the minutiae involved in processing a prospect's request.

The departments and labor services involved in inquiry management include:

1. Agencies: advertising, public relations, direct marketing, and online services agencies create demand through all of the traditional lead-generation tactics. They have an intense interest in the outcome.
2. Inbound telemarketing (taking toll-free calls), which typically reports to sales, marketing, or both.
3. Inquiry qualification departments. While the business rules governing the pursuit of a qualified lead varies,

these people will call inquirers to qualify and nurture them. In the process they eliminate students, competitors, and other illegitimate inquiries.

4. Outbound lead-generation department.
5. Inside sales.
6. Marketing.
7. Marketing communications.
8. Sales operations.
9. Field sales marketing managers.
10. Sales channel management.
11. Demand management department, which may report to sales or marketing. Also known as inquiry management department.
12. Data entry, which may be in sales or marketing.
13. Warehousing for collateral, which includes picking and packing literature packages (includes a letter, literature, technical data sheets, business reply device, dealer locations, etc.) and mailing literature.
14. Printing vendors: In addition to printing collateral, printers may warehouse and ship your literature individually or in bulk quantities to resellers.
15. Direct mail houses that may warehouse and ship your literature to inquirers or in bulk to resellers.
16. IT services: Internal for software hosting, report generation, programming for sales force automation and contact management.
17. IT services: External, including ASP software/services provider, sales force automation software, contact management, and CRM.
18. Outsourced inbound and outbound telemarketing facilities.
19. Outsourced bulk literature distribution faculties.
20. Inquiry management vendors. Includes advertising

agencies that do this work, plus printers, fulfillment vendors, and direct mail vendors that do it part-time.

21. International offices that may have to mimic the domestic operations for all of the above.

These departments are involved in:

1. Creating the inquiries in a manner that the company can accept (electronic, toll-free calls, business reply cards, reader service numbers from print magazines, lead forms manually completed by in-field reps or prospects, etc.

2. Receiving and sorting inquiries.

3. Data-entry of records: about 50% require manual data entry and 50% are now electronic direct from the inquirer via the Web, trade shows, direct mail landing pages, and contact centers.

4. Warehousing and inventory maintenance of literature.

5. Creation of literature packages (could run into hundreds of packages).

6. Assembly and mailing of literature packages.

7. Creation of electronic fulfillment packages and the content that goes into the "packages."

8. Screening for duplicate inquiries.

9. Screening for competitors.

10. Screening for previous inquirers (tracking: being able to view all those from the same company that have inquired in the past).

11. Grading the inquiry with the assignment of a "rank" to judge the inquiry source.

12. Nurturing of the inquiry if it is not sales ready: email, mail, and telephone.

13. Sales territory definitions: by zip codes, area code, county, country, product, distribution channel, product value, etc.

14. Sales lead distribution by sales territory or by product, by sales channel or any combination of these as in item 13 above.
15. Sales lead closure: reporting on the sales actions taken (closing the loop).
16. Reporting: marketing and sales report creation and distribution.
17. Accepting toll and toll-free calls from promotions.

I have found that companies that generate fewer than 300 inquiries per month can handle the inquiries in-house with part-time help from several departments. An off-the-shelf inquiry management software package is all they need. They will have trouble handling spikes in the volume of inquiries (for instance, inquiries from shows) and may require temporary help. But a small volume means that the normal month-to-month flow can be strong-armed with little effort by people who have other duties.

For more than 300 inquiries per month and (usually) a larger sales force or a greater number of sales channels and products, the equation becomes more complicated and the operations become more expensive to manage (labor and software). A dedicated staff is usually needed.

When I visit a company, I begin by asking the marketing manager how their inquiries are processed. I suggest that we take a walk around and ask the people doing the job what they do to manage the inquiry. The marketing manager will stop by the front desk and ask the receptionist what they do with the new inquiries. Here is a typical response:

Well, when I get enough of the inquiries, I normally sort them, maybe throw out the ones I can't read, and then pass them on to someone who does the data entry.

The data-entry person says:

I normally enter them into the system when I have enough, and then pass them along to fulfillment.

The fulfillment admin says:

As soon as I have enough of them, maybe once a week, I normally assemble them by product and pick the literature and stuff it for mailing.

The lead distribution person says:

When I get enough inquiries on a spreadsheet, I normally separate them by zip code and distribute them to the rep who covers that area.

The shipping person says:

Look, first I have to ship product. Whenever I can get to these literature packages, I get to them. I need enough of them to bother with. My job is to ship product.


A familiar pattern develops in these conversations. The code words "Normally" and "When I get enough" are common descriptors from the clerical work force. The issue is that for most companies the lead volume isn't great enough to have a full-time person just for sorting, data-entering, taking in-bound calls, printing letters for fulfillment, and picking and packing literature. Without a full-time person this important work becomes part-time work and part-time work gets done when people get around to it.

This pattern is alarming when the person who says the magic word "normally" is asked, "Show me the leads that you currently have to put through the system." Very often the person reaches into a drawer and rummages around in a pile of inquiries of indeterminate age. They look up to you with a sheepish smile and mutter something like, "I guess I'm a little behind right now. But I'll get these done right away. When I have time. When I have enough of them to warrant the effort."

The exceptions to this are the inquiries from your Web site or promotional landing pages. Because they are electronic, they do not need manual data entry and will often be driven directly into the software for screening and distribution to sales. The fulfillment may be delayed unless it is done electronically as a PDF file.

Most inquiries from non-Web sources move through the system in a slow-motion fashion that results in sales losses to competitors who show up first. If you allow people to process inquiries when they "get around to it," it will appear that marketing is doing a poor job of demand creation—whether they in fact are or not. And the salespeople won't have a prayer of making quota.

So how do you decide how much time, effort, and money should be put into managing the inquiry flow? The first consideration is the value of the product and the cost for managing the inquiry. You wouldn't think of spending $25 per inquiry to manage an inquiry for a $39 software product that can be bought at retail locations. Even $7 for fulfillment and lead distribution is too much for this product. But the same $25 for a $1,500 laptop computer, a $25,000 lift truck, a $7,500 stove, a $100,000 clinical chemistry analyzer, or a $75,000 ski boat is a good investment.

With the advent of large considered purchases in consumer markets—$10,000 home cooking systems, spas, pools, refrigeration systems, wine cellars, closet systems, garage flooring and cabinetry—inquiry management for B2C companies is becoming as important as it is for B2B.

The second consideration is how much control you exert over the sales channel and how the inquiry-management system will help close more sales (and thus earn back its cost). Will the salesperson report back on the resolution of an inquiry? With the use of Web-based systems to access information, even mom-and-pop resellers in rural locations have embraced sales-lead retrieval on the Web as a huge boon to their business. While inquiries have always been sent to resellers (usually by mail, email, fax, or spreadsheet), most of them didn't participate in two-way communications to tell the sponsoring company what happened to the inquiry. Now that it is easy to send a sales-lead resolution back to the manufacturer, the less sophisticated resellers are participating. If your products are sold at retail locations, sending inquiries to retailers is like pouring money down a well. Most of these retailers want participation from you in the form of dollars to create traffic and demand. Sometimes these "co-op dollars" at large retailers take on an aspect of a pay-to-play fee. But that is another story that could be a book in itself.

Let's review the three ways that inquiries can be managed based on a company's products and channels of distribution.

## Fulfill and Forget: Low Touch

Fulfill and forget inquiries are just that. Usually these are B2C but also low-cost B2B. Products are sold through retailers or distributors and resellers. The manufacturer advertises and typically drives inquirers to a Web site, a toll-free number, and/or most likely a retail establishment. The manufacturer's products are usually less than a few hundred dollars, the margins are small, and they don't control the sales channel. They advertise for name recognition (brand awareness) and to drive immediate need buyers into the retail store. Fulfillment is usually not done or is minimal, inquiries are not sent to the sales channel, and in some cases a database of inquirers is not even kept (not recommended).

The percentage of people who buy (anyone's product) is often more than 45%, and the time frame for a group of inquirers to buy is much less than a year and more likely a few weeks or a few months. The goal for these manufacturers is to create interest and drive the suspect into the reseller or retail store.

Salespeople dealing with this type of inquirer are closers. They sell on the spot on price and delivery. They repeatedly ask for the sale and are loathe to see the buyer walk away because they know that if they don't sell the person then and there, the sale will most likely and quickly go to someone else.

These types of inquiries have the following in common:

- Low cost products, less than $1,000.
- Multiple channels of distribution with little control over follow-up.
- Cost of fulfillment is a factor. A dollar is often too much for these manufacturers.
- Usually a high volume of inquiries.
- Follow-up is less important.
- Product information is available on the Web.
- Commodity sale.
- Perhaps the most important: The end user must know where to buy.

Response management for companies with these types of sales processes and channels means being sure that the potential buyer knows where to buy the product. Capturing the names and contact information for these inquirers has become an increasingly important goal for companies. The contact information can be vital for marketing managers trying to make quota in marketplaces where lists of potential buyers are difficult to find. Marketing ROI reports that tie marketing to sales are measured through special promotions or marketing research, such as Did You Buy studies that sample inquirers from different media.

## Considered Purchase:
## Continuous Touches, Some Nurturing

These are mostly B2B but includes some B2C considered purchasers. Considered purchase buyers are for products over $1,000 or products that are bought and frequently replaced so that the lifetime value (LTV) of a buyer is high. Inquirers in this group will feel compelled to contact the company, get information, and eventually speak with a salesperson who can educate them and help them make a decision.

These are not commodity products. It requires a salesperson who will answer more than simple price and delivery questions. The touches (steps) required to make the sale are as few as two or three but could be eight to twelve touches. The CMO (Chief Marketing Officer) Council in its 2004 survey says, "57 percent of survey respondents said it takes six months or less to close an average deal, but 48 percent said it takes from six months to one year or longer to close the typical deal."[1]

Touches include initial fulfillment, calls to qualify the inquirer's need, visits to discuss the inquirers need or pain, proposals, presentations to a large staff, building prototypes, negotiations with the buyer and with purchasing, and final delivery. In these instances, the inquiry request is fulfilled by marketing: The inquirer may be called for answers to additional qualification questions and then given to the salesperson for resolution. The Rule of 45 very much applies to these inquiries.

Salespeople in these situations take control of the sale, provide the necessary education, and expect to close an average sale in three to six months. They consult and give advice. While the products are not commodities, the average salesperson doesn't necessarily need an engineering degree or highly specialized formal training to be successful. They build up expertise in their product area and will ask for the sale less often than the commodity salesperson. These salespeople will take orders for many individual products each month and may sell a wide variety of products offered by the company. Typical products in this category include capital equipment of almost any description. There may be some involvement from system engineers or product specialists and other technical people to assist in the sale.

The common characteristics for these inquiries are:

- Products $1,000 +.
- Direct sales forces or loyal distribution.
- Cost of fulfillment not a factor, $3 to $14.
- Volume of inquiries: 300 to many thousands per month.
- Follow-up is very important.
- Fulfillment of mailed literature is common.
- Not a commodity product, but not quite a consultative sale.
- eMarketing is an option here to help in the touches.

Many marketers believe that qualification is just as important for these inquiries and that no one who is not sales-ready should be sent to a salesperson. The argument is often solved by the company's method of distribution. The more direct you sell, the more likely you will nurture inquirers. If you sell through distribution, you will most likely send all inquiries out, the good, the bad, and the ugly.

## Nurture Processing: Inquiries for Long, Technical Sales Cycles

The last group has a purchase price of $25,000 to millions of dollars and is almost exclusively in the domain of B2B. These sales inquiries fall into products sold by a consultative sales force. The sales cycle is long on these sales, typically 6 to 18 months or more. The Rule of 45 applies here, as it does for the Considered

Purchase Inquirers. A salesperson in this instance is truly consultative and probably has a technical degree or an advanced degree or equivalent work experience. The salesperson may be part of or a leader of a team of people that will satisfy this prospect.

Inquiries in this instance are "nurtured" by inside sales or a vendor and progress from initial literature fulfillment and qualification to a natural hand-off to the salesperson when the "time is right." The time may be right when the buyer says, "Now is the time to send in your Systems Consultant." This is when the salesperson begins to form a team of experts that he or she will need to satisfy this buyer.

The common characteristics for these inquiries are:

- Moderate to very expensive products: $25,000 +.
- Great for a controlled direct sales force but resellers can play a role here.
- Fulfillment and pursuit could go to $50 to $100 per inquiry.
- Volume is usually on the lower end: 300 to several thousand inquirers a month.
- Follow-up is a continuous, close-contact program. There are many, many touches.
- Fulfillment of mailed hard copy literature is common.
- This is a very much a consultative sale.
- Marketing will often, but not always, assume pursuit duties until the inquirer is ready to buy: telemarketing, mail, and email.
- eMarketing is an option to help in the touches.

Regardless of the situation you are in, you must address the requests of your prospects in a timely manner while moving the inquiry asset from the potential side of the ledger to the permanent customer side. In the next chapters we will review the ways you can manage the inquiry. We will look at managing inquiries in-house (and the software required to do that) and managing them outside with inquiry-management service providers.

## Actions to Take from This Chapter

1. Chart out step by step how you are managing inquiries and do a walk-about. Go to each person responsible for that step and ask them what their duties are. How often do they do what they are supposed to do for their part? Do you hear the word 'normally" from too many of the people?

2. Find out how you manage your inquiries and decide if you are:

   a. Fulfill and Forget

   b. Considered Purchase

   c. Nurture Processing

3. Are you exerting the right effort for the category in which you reside?

4. Are you acting like a fulfill and forget company when you should be nurture processing?

## *NOTE*

[1] CMO Council report, "Gauging the Cost of What's Lost, Improve the Return on Investment," 2004, page 10.

# 7 B2B Inquiries: Special Handling

As we look at marketing and sales stages, several big ugly questions arise that can cause a breakdown of the teamwork between marketing and sales. The questions are:

1. What is a qualified or sales-ready lead?
2. Should marketing attempt to qualify an inquiry before it is sent to sales?
3. Should nonqualified inquiries be withheld from sales?
4. Should anything other than hot inquiries be sent to sales?
5. If an inquiry doesn't reach a predetermined qualification stage, should it be nurtured until it is "sales ready"?
6. Who should "nurture" the inquirer?
7. If an inquiry doesn't reach a sales-ready stage, should it be thrown away?
8. Should salespeople only spend their time on the most qualified inquiries?

Some managers send every inquiry to sales regardless of grade or qualification. Others do not want to waste a salesperson's time by pursuing low-quality inquiries mixed in with high-probability buyers. While the Rule of 45 says that nearly half of all inquiries will turn into a sale for someone, finding out which half is the most difficult job for sales or marketing.

Everyone seems to have his or her own idea of a secret sauce to get the greatest yield from inquiries and the salespeople. I've heard:

> "I won't send an inquiry to my salespeople unless the person has reached a qualification level based on the answers to the questions I ask them. If I can't reach some of them, I'll toss the inquiries rather than have my salespeople spend time on unqualified prospects."

> "I send everything to my salespeople and I let them sort it out. That's their job. I know there are bad ones in there, but I'm not going to spend another twenty bucks an inquiry to find the few that are students and competitors. Besides, so many of the inquirers don't share their real buying intent. If I toss them, it's great a waste of marketing dollars."

If it weren't for my long-held belief that most inquirers lie about their intent, I could more easily buy into a strict policy of filtering to send only "sales-ready" leads to sales. The problem—a difficult one—is identifying when an inquirer is "sales ready," because there is no fail-safe process for determining "sales ready." Unfortunately, buyers always have the advantage and can hide their intent when qualification is only by mail, email, or telephone. If you want to squeeze the final drop of sales out of a group of inquiries, the salesperson is the person to do it, but his or her cost is much greater than the cost a of few calls, emails, and mailing to re-qualify an inquiry. People lie, mislead, intend to buy but don't, lose their budgets, quit their jobs, and go out of business. The waste is at least 55%. It takes a well-designed nurturing system to find just the golden 45% at just the time that they are sales ready. It looks good on paper, I've done it, but I always suspect that within the sawdust and scrap there are buyers.

Bill Herr, Managing Director of Sales Lead Development for CMP Media, LLC, with a long history of managing inquiries for hundreds of corporations when he worked for inquiry management vendors, has said that, "It is more important to get salespeople in front of prequalfied prospects rather than many unqualified or underqualified suspects who are a waste of a salesperson's time."[1]

However, this approach isn't foolproof because the filtering devices and nurturers by phone will still miss some of the buyers. Of course, there is a point of diminishing returns when a salesperson should abandon his or her efforts to convert a long-term inquirer if he has hotter, short-term buyers lined up with purchase orders in hand.

Ultimately the tough decision to nurture and only send 100% sales-ready, purchase-orders-in-hand, qualified leads and trash the rest will be decided by a few questions:

1. Do you have enough of a margin in the product you are trying to sell to spend $15 to $50 on nurturing?
2. Do you mind that some real buyers will be flushed?
3. How will the nurturing chore be done, who will do it, and how much will it add to the cost of the unqualified inquiries?

Nothing is 100%, but the buyers are there and nurturing works. Hundreds of Did You Buy studies conducted by a wide range of clients have consistently shown that 75% of those who inquire say they will buy something, but only 45% actually do purchase from someone. What about the remaining 30%? Of course, the clearly unqualified inquirers—competitors, students, and others—can be safely trashed. But of the rest, how many are serious prospects and potential buyers? How many prospects can you afford to give to your competitors? When is it more efficient to track down a lukewarm or even cold inquiry rather than leave it, as a possible sale, to a competitor?

The decision to send only qualified inquirers or all inquirers to your sales reps can only be made if you understand the steps in the decision-making process. Creating a process flowchart or process map is helpful in deciding how this should work in your organization. The process map and the steps for the management of inquiries must reflect the specific nature of the product and the kind of sale, so it will vary from company to company.

As discussed in Chapter 6, the more expensive and complicated the product, the more likely that the process of conversion will be longer and need more and more defined steps. Each of the steps is a stage, and inquirers will spend time in the stages as they are worked upon (or nurtured) by marketing and sales. At each stage inquirers are filtered out (found to be either unqualified to buy or to have bought someone else's product), moved ahead to the next stage, or moved out because they bought your product and completed the process in your favor. The steps can typically be divided into marketing and sales process stages. To create the stages you need marketing and sales in the same room for a few hours to ask these key questions:

1. Marketing: Asking profile questions of the buyer's intentions is the first filtering stage for sales. What are the most important questions you want asked of the inquirer?
2. What are your stages in processing a name for distribution to the salespeople?
3. Sales: Tell us how many stages you have in the sales process.

Once done, you will have developed your basic stages, which can be refined. Developing these stages means mapping out the process stages that your typical buyer takes. These stages will be different and should be taken into account as part of your solutions. With these two processes defined within "swim lanes" on a chart, you can make some decisions on how the inquiry-management process can contribute to sales. The following section reviews the basic marketing and sales stages and how a typical process map takes shape.

## Marketing and Sales Stages

In the most sophisticated companies sales and marketing departments have divided the inquiry life cycle process into Marketing Qualification Stages and Sales Stages because it encourages marketers (and others in the company) to think of marketing as a process that can be controlled and guided if they qualify inquiries before giving them to sales. Sales departments have created their sales stages to track the probability of an opportunity becoming a sale. These sales stages are more commonly known as pipeline, funnel, or deal stages. It has only been in recent years that sales and marketing have come together to connect the initial inquiry qualification stage with the sales stages and map out a total process.

Regardless of the number of stages or the terms used to describe them, some companies may have a dozen or more marketing and sales stages. After an inquiry arrives and is graded, it should be entered into a process that takes it from birth to death.

## Marketing Qualification Stages

Once inquiries have been accepted into the company by marketing—the company has eliminated the duplicates, has gotten rid of competitor inquiries, has checked to see if the person has inquired on the same product in the last 30 days, and has dropped the inquiries from Mickey Mouse and Donald Duck— they can then be graded according to the applicable business rules. They will emerge as either suspects or prospects. Suspects are considered unqualified inquiries, and prospects are those that have reached a higher level of confidence so that their potential for a near-term sale can be taken seriously.

The marketing manager has two choices. One, he can send the unqualified suspect to the salesperson and let him or her deal with it. Two, he can send it into a nurture process and withhold the inquirer from the sales team until it is qualified and is considered a prospect or declared dead (see Exhibit 7.1).

- **Suspect:** Nothing is known about a suspect except name, company, address, and product of interest. There are few

---

**EXHIBIT 7.1**
**Marketing Process Prior to Inquiry Distribution**

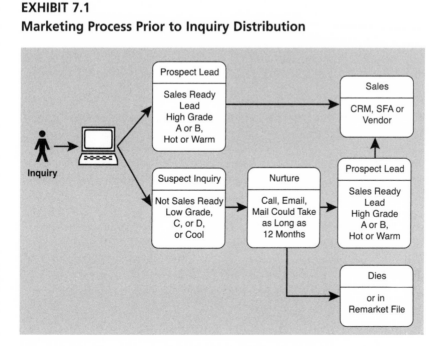

answers to profile questions that qualify this person so they receive a low numerical grade level, a letter grade of C or D, or a low temperature rating of cool or cold. These inquiries are often from advertising and public relations sources where you can't ask questions in order to understand the prospects needs. If a person sees your advertisement or press release and circles a reader service number, you will most likely get the least information concerning a suspect's propensity to buy. Be careful not to call these kinds of inquirers "unqualified." While that may be an apt description, unqualified to the salespeople will often translate into nonbuyers who are not worth their time to follow up. And you do want them to follow up to determine whether the inquirer is indeed a nonbuyer or an active prospect.

- **Prospect:** This person has answered profile questions in a positive manner and has attained a high numerical grade— a grade B level or higher, or a temperature grade of hot or warm. Sometimes prospects are interchangeable with the term *qualified*. Regardless, the prospect is a person who has answered profile questions, so that you can screen the person's need sufficiently to understand their intent to buy and their degree of seriousness. These are called *qualified inquiries*.

- **Nurture Stage:** This is where low-level suspects (not a sufficiently high grade level to be called a lead) are sent. Nurturing is done by:
  a. An inside lead qualification department; this can be marketing and telemarketers that pursue, qualify and nurture the inquiry until the person says, "Send in your salesperson."
  b. Inside sales.
  c. An outside inquiry management/telemarketing vendor.

- **Dead:** An inquiry can be dead on arrival in marketing for many reasons, **but** by going through the nurture stage, it is found to be a nonbuyer. Resolution designations are used at this stage to close out the inquiry and to give it a final grade for marketing reports. We cover the resolution codes later but most of them are:

1. No interest.
2. Information only.
3. Could not contact.
4. Bought other (could happen before sales can reach them).
5. Remarket: worth going into a file for on-going communications.

In most instances about 25% of the inquiries are screened out and never reach the salesperson. Of course, the majority of inquiries will die later—in the sales stages—but it also can happen earlier—in marketing. If it dies later in the sales stages, the prospect bought from a competitor or didn't make a decision.

## Sales Stages: Funnel, Opportunity, Deal, or Pipeline

Once the lead is sent to the salesperson, it begins to go through a filtering process that will either kill it as a prospect or advance it to the next level of the pipeline. These stages can be just a few or a dozen or more. Every company and its products are different. The basic stages are here, but others can be added.

- **Sales Lead, aka Sales-Ready Lead.** This is truly a qualified inquiry. They have an immediate need, a budget, a projected time frame for purchase, and usually a few other "custom" thresholds that have been reached so that it is a genuine sales lead.
- **Discovery.** Many inquiries never get past the discovery

**EXHIBIT 7.2**

**Sales Stages: Every Company has Different Stages**

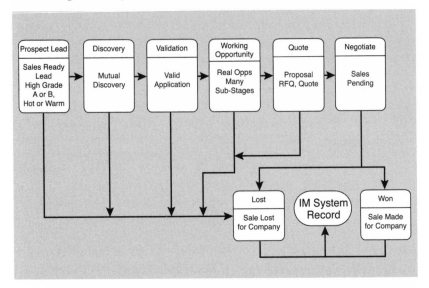

stage. This is where the people and the companies decide if they want to work together and if the products fit the need. Discovery happens during the first few meetings, where the prospect and the seller size each other up and get the problems fully fleshed out. This is where the chemistry so vital to any successful sale must happen; otherwise, the future deal dies here.

- **Validation.** At this stage the proof of concept begins to assert itself. Whether it is through a demonstration, free trial, free sample, Web seminar, reference checks, etc., validation is the stage where someone has to finally say, "Yep, I think this will work the way we need it to."

- **Working Opportunity.** Just what it says, this lead is being worked by the sales representative and has an opportunity to become a sale or to at least move to the next sales stage. An opportunity is most often those names that are transferred into the sales rep's contact system (SFA). These are the leads that appear in the salesperson's forecast. Not every lead that knocks on your door is worthy of making it to the forecast; probably, at best, 50%. The huge mistake many companies make is dumping all inquiries into the SFA system and then trying to manage the database, which is bloated with all sorts of irrelevant names and information, at the salesperson's level.

- **Proposal.** Whether it is a quote or a proposal, 1 page or 50 pages, somewhere in the process a number will have to be given to the buyer. Every company should know the closing ratio of its proposals. Once that proposal is laid on the prospect's desk you should know within a narrow percentage what your chances are.
- **Negotiation/Sale Pending.** Maybe we're slicing this too thinly, but some companies know that the negotiation stage can take time. Once in this area the outcome is reasonably predictable. Unless the salesperson has not done his homework or the two companies have not properly identified any serious outstanding issues, the outcome should not be in question; only the final value and terms and conditions are being discussed.

A company can choose additional sales stages that match their particular needs for forecasting. With some foresight the sales stages will have been identified that match the prospect's buying stages. If the two match and sales tools are created to help the salesperson sell and close at each stage, so much the better.

In later chapters we will discuss the final resolution of the prospect in the pipeline and what those resolutions should be called.

The discussion of stages and processes and process mapping begins an in-depth discussion of Six Sigma as it pertains to sales and marketing. A great site for additional information on Six Sigma in sales and marketing is: www.isixsigma.com.

## Actions to Take from This Chapter

1. Define a qualified lead for your organization.
2. Will you send only qualified leads to the field?
3. How will you nurture those that are not qualified?
4. What are the marketing stages for inquiries?
5. What are the sales stages for inquiries?

### *NOTE*

[1] Bill Herr, Speaker at the DMA Advanced B-to-B Seminar: *Building High Performance B-to-B Lead Generation*, June 2005.

# 8 In-House or Outsource?

## Pluses and Minuses

The great majority of companies, probably close to 90%, manage inquiries in-house. If you have a consistent influx of inquiries week to week and fewer than 300 inquires a month, in-house is controllable. Above 300 inquiries per month the process often begins to be expensive, and things seem to fall apart. Inquiry spikes delay the processing. Getting inquiries sent to the field is sporadic. Literature isn't sent immediately and reports are scarce. The old system of inquiries being processed is slowed more often because low numbers of inquiries are usually a part-time job for someone (or many someones). When the numbers get higher and salespeople begin to complain, when spreadsheet lead distribution becomes cumbersome, the company may turn to outside services rather than increase the headcount just to properly manage leads.

If you can afford to manage inquiries in-house, there can be definite advantages:

- The sales lead manager for the company feels that they have tight control of the processes because everything is on-site.
- Depending on the volume of inquiries, the manager feels

that it is less costly to perform these functions in-house with people who can "do the data entry, pick and pack, mailing, lead distribution and creating reports."

- The company may already have an SFA or CRM software program with the ability to manage the distribution and reporting of the inquiry.

The disadvantages to managing inquiries in-house are:

- Software programs for these functions are often on a subscription model and per-seat license fees are not inexpensive. The programs for inquiry management are commonly an after-thought module on an SFA or CRM system. There is frequently a yearly maintenance and upgrade fee.
- The software requires IT time to manage the application. Getting some reports involves an IT or a systems administrator, and they are not pleased with having to create special report functions or turn out reports.
- There may be slow times for some employees dedicated to inquiry management if the inquiry volume is not consistent. Senior management does not like having idle hands.
- The company may have to hire temporary labor in peak times. This labor is used for entering inquiries into the system, picking and packing literature, or calling suspects that are unqualified.
- Companies with CRM systems may not want to open their company up to resellers to use their CRM system, or pay for a per seat fee for an application service provider solution. Inquiries, therefore, may end up in emails and spreadsheets with no accountability.
- The person managing the process is usually an entry-level manager who is sequestered in one department with little or no authority over the people in the other departments who "help" him (or her) manage the process. This person also has no authority over anyone regarding follow-up.

- There is no single champion for the whole process, start to finish, over all of the employees who touch every inquiry. There is often open conflict between the departments without a senior champion.

Companies that retain the inquiry management function in-house usually:

- Have very large sales forces or resellers and a large volume of inquiries, and hiring a staff to do this full time is not a burden.
- Have products that cost only a few hundred dollars or less.
- Have a low volume of inquiries. The products may be B2B or B2C. Fulfillment is often not needed. These companies do not feel they have the margin, the need, or the volume of inquiries for the detailed management of the inquirer. Their philosophy is, "Tell 'em where to buy it and let's move on."
- Have a very high volume of inquiries (and often a low purchase price), and "fulfill and forget" is all they can afford. These are often consumer products where the point of purchase is well known by the end user and notifying sales reps isn't necessary. Low-cost software applications are often used.
- Have small sales forces, and distributing leads and fulfilling literature requests isn't difficult.

The most common trait among these companies is that their marketplaces are not necessarily small but controllable and that tracking the inquiries they get is not difficult to fulfill and distribute to the sales force. While laborious, systems using spreadsheets for reporting on lead closures work for many small companies. Unfortunately, the salespeople feel that even when they fill out the resolution of an inquiry in the spreadsheet, no one is looking at it. No one cares. They think that management wants them to fill out forms as just another make-work exercise and that no actions will be taken from their labor. While pulling information about sales-lead resolution by source from spreadsheets isn't difficult, it isn't something managers tend to "get-around-to." Most managers who work without a closed-loop system have the nagging feeling that should anyone ask them to justify their marketing budget they would come up empty.

## Criteria for Making the Decision

One of the key factors that should be considered in deciding whether to go outside or stay in-house is understanding the cost for doing it in-house. Look at the functions across all departments, put a cost figure on each of those functions, and total it up. There is no "right" or "wrong" decision. There is only a control-versus-cost decision.

The spreadsheet in Exhibit 8.1 shows the common functions of inquiry management in-house. It is a good place to start estimating your own in-house costs. The estimates for an hourly cost in column B should adjusted to reflect your circumstances. (Ignore functions not performed in your operation.) This estimate shows an inquiry volume of 10,000 per year with 50 sales territories and 100 pieces of literature. This example does not take into account multiple mails or emails as part of a nurture strategy; it only includes telemarketing nurture calls (average of three). This might be considered a typical B2B company.

## Software Providers for In-House Systems

To avoid confusion between pure-play inquiry management software and ASP, CRM, and SFA products, let's look at the definitions and differences between and among these overused acronyms.[1]

- ASP (Application Service Provider): a hosted software contractor. An ASP operates/distributes software from its data center, which customers access online under a service contract.

- CRM (Customer Relationship Management): a software program that is customer-centric. The main goals are to optimize revenue through greater customer satisfaction by means of improved interactions at each customer touch point. This is accomplished by an understanding of customer needs, based on their buying patterns and demographics.
- SFA (Sales Force Automation): information systems used in marketing and management that automate some sales and sales force management functions. Very few companies want to be known as Sales Force Automation products. Rightly or not, they prefer the term CRM.

Pure-play inquiry management software companies (versus SFA or CRM applications) are generally small companies (under $50 million in revenue) that have developed niche applications for managing B2B inquiries. The company that buys the software must have an IT person(s) who can help manage the application and an administrator who makes sure inquiries are entered into the data- management system and distributed, literature packages are fulfilled (labels pulled, literature picked and packed), leads distributed (on the Web, paper, fax, email, etc), and reports created for marketing and sales. Some companies completely manage this function in-house as well as any vendor. It just takes software, disciplined people, and money. If the volume is large enough (over 10,000 inquiries a year), it may be possible to fund this process in-house less expensively than doing it outside. That's why you need to run the numbers.

The "other" type of software provider is sales force automation (SFA) software and CRM (customer relationship management) software. For many years SFA people have said that they manage sales leads along with account and contact information that the salespeople enter into the system separate from sales leads.

**EXHIBIT 8.1**

**Estimate for Managing 10,000 Inquiries In-House with Telemarketing Qualification.**

**Annual Inquiry Handling Cost**

| Cost Drivers<br>Labor | Inquiry Volume:<br>Territories<br>SKUs<br>Rate/Unit Cost | 10,000<br>50<br>100<br>Hours/Mon. Cost | Extended Cost |
|---|---|---|---|
| Receiving and sorting inquiries (average 3 minutes each) | $ 10 | 41.7 | $ 5,000 |
| Data Entry (20 records per hour) | $ 10 | 41.7 | $ 5,000 |
| Inquiry Distribution (100 records per hour) | $ 10 | 8.3 | $ 1,000 |
| Territory Management (75% of territories need changes) | $ 12 | 3.13 | $ 450 |
| Inventory Maintenance: each SKU counted 2x | $ 14 | 25 | $ 4,200 |
| Receiving literature and stocking shelves (1.5 hours ea.) | $ 14 | 12.5 | $ 2,100 |
| Literature Fulfillment (20 per hour) | $ 14 | 41.7 | $ 7,000 |
| Report Generation: enter actual | $ 15 | 5 | $ 900 |
| Temporary Labor (peak flow) 6 times a year x 40 hours | $ 15 | 20 | $ 3,600 |
| Management (X hours a month) | $ 40 | 25 | $ 12,000 |
| Mailing Labor (one hour per day) | $ 8 | 21 | $ 2,016 |
| Telemarketing Outbound qualification calls (50% of leads) | $ 13 | 5000 | $ 21,667 |
| Telemarketing Inbound 800# 5x12 hours of coverage | $ 13 | 252 | $ 39,312 |

| | | | |
|---|---|---|---|
| Telemarketing Management (1 FTE for 4 TSRs) | $ 25 | 160 | $ 48,000 |
| Telemarketing nurture after qualification (75% of inquiries) | $ 13 | $ 1,875 | $ 22,500 |
| Telco Costs @$2.50 (42 minutes at $.6 cents a minute) | | 139 | $ 4,167 |
| Benefits @ X% of total labor cost | 22% | | $ 33,032 |
| **Labor Cost** | | | **$ 211,943** |
| | | | |
| **Equipment** | | | |
| Computer(s): New every four years | $ 2,500 | | $ 625 |
| Cost of work areas: desk, tables, chairs, racks | $ 5,000 | | $ 500 |
| | | | |
| **Space** | | | |
| Office and literature storage areas: Sq/Ft | $ 1.25 | 3000 | $ 45,000 |
| **Equipment and Space** | | | $ 46,125 |
| **Total** | | | **$ 256,943** |
| | | | |
| **Cost per Inquiry Managed** | | | **$ 26** |

The strengths of SFA include the extensive client information available through extremely robust databases plus the program's ability to enable the user to control daily sales processes (calendar), including call-backs, notes, setting appointments, and tracking pipeline stages/sales forecasts. There is a difference, however, between managing inquiries, tracking a campaign's return on investment from its lead-generating programs, and managing contacts with pipeline reporting.

The important criteria for evaluating a program (whether it's called SFA or CRM) involves the ability to manage the following sample operation without significant additional cost:

1. The company has one sales force of 50 selling 15 different products in the enterprise space. Leads are distributed by zip code.

2. Another sales group of 100 sells the 15 products from item one above (for products valued less than $15,999) plus another 85 products into the mid-market. Leads are distributed by zip code.

3. An inside sales group of 100 sells the 85 products from item 2 above plus another 25 products to the marketplace of fewer than 100 employees. Leads are distributed by telephone area code.

4. There also are 750 dealers who work with the sales group from item 2 and get their leads assigned by the sales reps from that group.

5. And then there are the four people who sell to OEM corporations for specially-made products that are customized for specific one-off applications.

6. The number of literature SKUs is over 400, including accessories and specialty items, and there is a need for accurate monthly inventory tracking, including all SKUs.

7. Lastly there are the 5 salespeople who work the national

accounts area and have grandfathered large accounts for products across all business units. These must be flagged regardless of zip codes or product designations and be sent to the national accounts manager.

Take this complicated sales structure and throw in the "spice" of a 20% turnover in sales territories and a 10% to 15% changeover in products, and you now have the reason why so many large companies go outside for this service, especially considering inquiry flow is sporadic. Many software programs can perform all of these functions, and as each year passes the programs are getting easier to work with and are becoming increasingly flexible with respect to complicated lead distribution. Regardless of the company or the software, get it in writing. Do not assume that inquiry management is a minor part of the program and that it will be covered later.

None of this is to say that many companies don't manage inquiries inside successfully. All it takes is the required staff and the necessary software program.

## Taking It Outside

Outsourcing has always been attractive, and with the advent of application service provider (ASP) programs, it is becoming easier. If, however, your company already has a contact management, SFA, or CRM system in place, be sure that your inquiry management vendor is capable of working with your existing software (does all of the labor and sends electronic records to be downloaded into your existing system). There are exceptions today whereby a company does not have one of these three prospect management systems already installed. If this is the case, the customer will use the vendor's lead delivery system. The companies that take customer acquisition management outside do it to:

- Avoid the headcount to database, fulfill, track sales territories, etc.
- Do not want to install specialized software programs on their computers throughout the organization.
- Have a need to allow access to the lead-management system for resellers. Resellers are often not invited to use the company's CRM or SFA system.

They have the following common characteristics:

- The company has more than 300 inquiries per month to tens of thousands.
- The products are generally high-tech products that cost over $1,000. The higher the value of the product, the more likely the company is to spend $10 to $50 per inquiry to completely manage and track the life cycle of the inquiry.
- The products can also be large considered-purchase B2C products with a high volume of inquiries (30,000 +).
- The company has a large sales force or channel of distribution—usually more than 25 direct salespeople or channels of distribution with a cast of hundreds or thousands.
- The company does not want to dedicate potentially as many as 20 employees just to manage the inquiries.
- The company does not want to burden its IT department, which dislikes managing another software application on everyone's computer.

## Inquiry Management Service Providers

I estimate the business for response management *service* firms at approximately $250 million. This estimate excludes software-only companies that sell inquiry management software, sales force automation, or CRM products that are meant to use their database abilities not only for inquiry management but also for the full range of contact management and customer relationship management needs of business-to-business corporations.

Service firms, for the most part, use a Web-based application service provider (ASP) model and supply various à la carte labor functions to manage the inquiry. These companies:

- Store literature and electronic files for hard copy and e-fulfillment.
- Accept inquiries in all formats and enter the names and profiles into a database system.
- Follow the business rules of their client to:
  —Fulfill the information request.
  —Distribute the inquiry to the proper salesperson or sales channel (usually via the Web, but also by mail, fax, and email).
  —Accept inbound toll-free calls.
  —Create sales-ready leads by performing outbound calls to qualify inquirers before the names and their needs are passed to the salespeople.
  —Use email and mail to drip irrigate or nurture inquirers until they are ready to speak to a salesperson from the sponsoring company.
  —Database the salesperson's resolution of the inquiry: Bought (from who), could not contact, not qualified, bought from competitor, future possibility, etc.
  —Provide the company's management team with relevant reports showing not simply sales follow-up but how many sales occurred from a particular source, source type, sales territory, etc. These reports include campaign data for the results of specific lead-generation programs.

Vendor corporations that perform these services on a fee basis can range from those firms that specialize in the business of response management to advertising or direct marketing agencies that run database programs or even printers that have gone into the bulk literature storage and distribution business, which often includes inquiry management. The costs of these services vary widely, depending on the company doing them, the sophistication of the systems they use to manage your inquiries, and the amount of account management time they expend on your behalf.

The advantages of managing inquiries outside are:

1. In the majority of cases, the companies will only charge a per inquiry fee. If you have few inquiries, you will pay less. More inquiries means you will pay more.
2. The really good vendors that specialize in this business can do it less expensively than most companies can do it with a staff of full-time employees.
3. There are generally no license fees or per seat costs from most of the vendors.
4. There is usually nothing installed on your computers or the salespeople's laptops. Your IT department is not called upon to install and maintain an inquiry-management application across the network.
5. Program improvements and management are not charged as a yearly maintenance and upgrade fee. Program improvements are expected at no cost.
6. The company does not have to dedicate people or space to this function, only someone to manage and oversee it.

The disadvantages are:

1. Control for the function resides with the vendor, though this can also be an advantage.
2. The database resides outside. This can be a threat if the vendor does not have a sufficient backup and recovery system.

3. Inquiries may be lost by the vendor. It doesn't happen very often with a reputable vendor who has checks and balances, but it can happen.
4. Costs may not be as predictable as an inside department. If inquiry volume increases, your costs will go up.

The cost for managing the inquiries at a vendor can be divided into:

1. Program start-up fees. These range from $5,000 to $50,000, with the majority being in the low teens. Start-up fees include:

- Customization of the computer program.
- Loading in sales territories.
- Creation of the business rule set that will determine how inquiries are distributed to the sales channel.
- Creation of literature packages (for example a 9"×12" envelope, cover letter, business reply card, product brochure, technical data sheets, price list, list of distribution, etc.).
- Accepting, counting, and storing literature.
- Creation of electronic fulfillment packages.
- Determining data transfer protocols, if any.
- Training salespeople and marketing people on the use of the system.
- Creation of nurturing program if appropriate:
  i. Mailers
  ii. Calling scripts
  iii. Email campaigns
- Scripting and training of inbound contact center people to take calls or answers emails.
- Scripting and training of outbound lead qualification people in the call center.

2. Inquiry processing fees. These fees can vary depending on the amount of time and labor that are spent on them. For instance:

- Inquiries that have hard-copy fulfillment.
- Inquiries without hard-copy fulfillment.
- Inquiries with an electronic fulfillment package.
- Inquiries that require a person to data enter the name, address, and profile information (for example, leads from trade shows, business reply cards, reader service numbers, etc).
- Inquiries that enter from electronic media such as Web sites, computer disks from trade shows, seminars, etc.
- Inquiries that require a wide range of nurturing over extended periods of time before the inquiry is sent to the salesperson.

3. Program management time. The outside firm will place your account under the supervision of a professional customer services manager. These experts advise the client on how they can reduce their cost for managing inquiries and increase sales though the efficient management of the inquiry. This is the person who makes sure that sales territories are maintained and updated, literature packages are changed and created, invoices are correct, telemarketing scripts are changed, special mailings are sent, literature is printed on demand, etc. They post and review reports, train new sales and marketing people on the system, and make sure that salespeople are happy with the system.

4. Telemarketing fees. Most inquiry management firms take inbound promotional toll-free calls for the client and often make outbound calls to qualify those inquiries that are not "qualified."

5. Postage fees. Most companies request a "postage deposit"

equal to two- to three-months' worth of the projected cost of the postage for the fulfillment packages. The inquiry management firm then invoices the client for the postage on a monthly basis.

Exhibit 8.2 is a checklist for managing inquiries. It can be a very helpful guide to making that all-important decision whether to keep inquiry management in-house or to outsource, and it can be used to evaluate software or service vendors.

---

**EXHIBIT 8.2**
**Checklist for Managing Inquiries: What Services Do You Require?**

*Cost*

Program start-up costs including customization

Monthly minimum

Cost per inquiry

Per seat license

*Capturing Inquirer's Interest*

Import of existing inquirer databases

Automated lead capture: from Web

Electronic lead capture: transfers, from shows, etc.

Manual data entry done in one business day or less

Capture of screening/qualification data: questions and answers

Inbound contact center services

*Special Identification Services*

Identification of key accounts: could be national or grandfathered
   accounts

(Continued)

---

**EXHIBIT 8.2  (Continued)**

Identification of competitor inquiries

Identification of previous inquirers

Identification of duplicate inquiries

Web site hosting: contact pages, etc.

*Fulfillment Services*

Hard copy literature fulfillment

Personalized laser letters

Email fulfillment: PDF files

A series of nurturing emails sent with content at
predetermined intervals

Follow-up hard copy fulfillment at predetermined intervals

Cost for receiving literature

Cost for literature inventory

International fulfillment

*Qualification & Ranking Services*

Follow-up email qualification of raw inquiries

Outbound telemarketing lead qualification of raw inquiries

Follow-up qualification mailings of raw inquiries

Lead ranking to identify sales readiness

*Inbound Telemarketing Services*

Cost for program start-up to include script and training

Cost for call center management

Cost per call (by the minute, by the call?)

Hours/coverage? 24/7 , 5/12 or _____

*Sales Lead Distribution*

Lead distribution to sales force within 24 hours
(within minutes is now common)

Supports business rules for distribution: direct, indirect,
by product, zip codes, area code, counties, states, etc.

Lead distribution to sales force via Internet,
email, fax, or hard copy

Automated key account assignment (national or
grandfathered accounts)

The ability for resellers to "chose and claim ownership"
of an inquirer

System to "pull back" an inquiry if it is not followed-up
within a specific time

Reminder emails to the sales channel if an inquiry
has not been opened within a specific time


*Nurturing Services*

Email nurturing

Cost for email nurturing service

Outbound call nurturing

Cost per outbound call (can include a per minute cost if applicable)

Cost for scripting

Cost for call center personnel training (per hour)

Cost for outbound call center management (hourly fee)


*Sales Follow Up & Opportunity Management*

Sales stage tracking

Sales resolution tracking/"Close the Sales Loop"

Collaborative information sharing (sharing inquiry access with others)

Pre-written online sales letters available on demand

(Continued)

---

**EXHIBIT 8.2 (Continued)**

*Reporting*

ROI reporting (not just revenue but percentage ROI)

Dashboard reporting

Campaign reporting: by source, source type

Projected sales amount

Sales pipeline reporting

Forecasts by rep, region, retail store, direct sales force

Market Intelligence Report: lost sales and won reports

Forecasting by source

Export sales and marketing reports

Bar and pie charts—online and downloadable

Lead distribution report for sales management

Lead aging reports (30, 60, 90 days)

Sales action reports by country, region, or sales territory

List of inquirers on demand by zip, rep, product, sold,
   lost, qualification, etc.

Cost for custom report creation (usually an hourly figure)

*Account Management*

What is the hourly cost for account management?

What percentage of the total monthly invoice is estimated to be
   account management?

*Technology*

Database access—downloadable on demand?

Ability to integrate with existing applications: SFA, Contact
   Management, CRM?

Any IT resource required?
_____

If an ASP model, guaranteed up-time?
_____

Yearly upgrade costs?
_____

Yearly warranty costs?
_____

License per seat?
_____

IT hourly program costs?
_____

Database limitations? Refers to number of records stored.
_____

## Actions to Take from This Chapter

1. Document how you are currently managing inquiries:
   a. Cost
   b. Follow-up and resolution
   c. ROI reporting
2. For documenting the cost for managing inquiries in-house, use Exhibit 8.1.
3. If you would like to use an SFA or CRM software program to manage your inquiries, make sure you dig deeply into the variables for this process before accepting the answer from the vendor, "Oh, yes, we manage inquiries, it's all included." All programs are not alike. Just because it costs more doesn't mean it can do what you need done. Use the checklist in Exhibit 8.2 and add your requirements to it.

## *NOTE*

[1] www.definethat.com

# ⑨ Inquiry Leakage

The subject of this chapter is probably the main reason for this book. I've mentioned this subject before and I'm going to mention it again because it involves the very survival of your company. Inquiry leakage is hurting most companies. Inquiries enter a company from many disparate places. Prospective buyers call, write, email, respond to campaigns, attend trade shows, and their names and interest are often lost. It happens when they call customer service or local sales offices, send emails to Web sites, send snail mail to anonymous addresses, and attempt to communicate in a dozen other ways, but they fail. Their names and needs are not captured. They beg for attention.

Leakage happens because most companies, unfortunately, are not counting all of the inquiries they receive, nor are they attributing the inquiries to their proper sources. Sometimes they are contacted, and sometimes they are lost and ignored. No one really intends to ignore a potential customer, but without a system to capture every name at every potential point of entry into the company, leakage just happens.

When this occurs, the marketing department will lose the ability to properly credit the lead-generating campaign that caused the person to make a contact. This isn't a small problem; it's a big problem. It's a "10% to 30% problem." Most companies that gain control of the portals of sales lead entry into their company see a 10% to 30% increase in inquiries and qualified leads that can be accurately counted and properly attributed to campaigns. Sales increase.

## Typical Points of Inquiry Leakage

The common areas of leakage are:

- **Calls to customer service.** Inquiry calls to this group are often thought of as intrusions and irritants. Customer service reps are seldom trained to determine what prompted the inquirer to call. They rarely have inquiry entry screens on their computers for this purpose. Even a paper form for taking inquiry interest is better than nothing. If your toll-free number in an advertisement could end up in customer service, get the operators trained on taking inquiry calls. Tell them how important these calls are for the company. Most inquiry management programs, including CRM, SFA, and contact management programs, have a section entitled, "Enter New Inquiry." Teach customer service people how to use it. Use paper as a backup or a last resort to capture the vital information of an inquirer, including the source.
- **Inquirers (usually callers) that go to a salesperson or local office.** In some companies inquiries are intentionally directed to the local sales office. That would be great, were it not for the fact that few of these offices will take the time to attribute the caller to a specific marketing campaign. Instead, the calls should be taken at a central contact center where the name and information is entered and then hot-transferred to the proper salesperson.
- **Calls to executives or marketing.** These are often lost for accountability purposes. Sometimes they are given to salespeople; sometimes the questions are answered, but the names and sources of the inquiry are not recorded.

Executives can also learn to use the "Enter New Prospect" screen.

- **Trade show inquiries.** Just because a sales rep speaks to someone in his or her territory during the show doesn't mean that he has the right to pocket the inquiry. Use computer lead retrieval or multiple-copy lead forms at shows and let the salesperson take a copy if it is in their area.
- **Emails from "Contact Us" Web pages.** Too often the emails that are generated go to someone who will read them or maybe forward them—but never add them to a database. They are not counted as an inquiry. Maybe the person's needs are met, maybe not. In the section that follows I will discuss capturing Web-page responses.
- **Small local shows.** After all, it is a local show. Why send the inquiries to the home office just so the representative can get them back a week later? The reason is that a local show may not be booked next year if the marketing department can't review the total quantity of inquiries and the ROI from this year's show. In addition, the prospect may not get the literature they wanted. Again, use multiple-copy lead forms so the reps can separate and keep their own copy.
- **International inquiries.** Too often inquires from foreign countries are not recorded. If they are, the names are many times not passed to the local sales office in the country or region that handles the prospect. They are lost.
- **Representative-generated inquiries.** One of the most under-counted sources of inquiries is the category called Rep Generated. It can be 5% to 10% of your total inquiry count if you:
    —Give the salesperson training on why they need to report these inquiries.
    —Give them an easy-to-use system to enter the names. Again these are entered in the "Enter New Prospect" sec-

tion of the inquiry management, CRM, SFA, or contact management program.

If you can stop the leakage, send all leads and inquiries through a single portal for counting and accountability, you will see an increase in sales. But, few reps make a living off the inquiries generated just from corporate. They have to attend networking meetings and even cold call. When they do, they should be able to enter the names in a database so that literature is sent, and then the names can be tracked. Give your salespeople a form or a place that they can go to and make this happen.

You now know that you must funnel all inquiries through a single counting process so that none leak away. Let's look at why you must allow the prospect to contact you in the manner that *they* want to use rather than the way you want them to contact you.

## Allowing the Prospect to Reach You Their Way

The goal of lead generation is simple: Get the greatest response from your marketing efforts by offering the prospect the ability to contact you in any manner they choose. You can't try to funnel everyone to the Web because you want it that way. If the person reading your advertisement or direct mail piece isn't next to their computer, they will most likely fill out the reply card or pick up the phone and dial your toll-free number. But if you haven't used a reply card or placed a toll-free number in a prominent place on your direct mail piece, the potential customers will say to themselves, "I'll get to them later." Later never comes for most inquirers.

For instance, a client was finalizing her new direct mail campaign and she had no business reply card in the package or toll-free number in the copy. The only way a prospect could respond was through their Web site URL with an extension. She had mailed a similar piece with essentially the same offer in the previous quarter. The results were low, and yet she and the direct mail company were going to try essentially the same piece with a different offer (when in doubt, change the offer, right?). I convinced her that maybe it wasn't just the offer but their use of the Web as the only point of entry, which gave people only one way to respond. Without an 800 number, a business reply card, or a landing site that was specific to the campaign (inquirers often drop the extension on the site address), she couldn't accurately identify who responded. She may have seen a bump in her Web site traffic over a two- or three-week period, but there was no hard proof of what caused the increase.

Taking my advice, she put a business reply card into the new mail package, used an 800 number, and directed people to a simple landing site URL, which was specific to the campaign. She created as many portals as possible and counted every inquiry that came through the doors she had opened. Her agency complained about having to insert the business reply card (cost and delay), plus the room needed for the 800 number in the copy and on the reply card. The agency didn't mind creating the special landing site.

Much to her surprise and to that of the agency, the response was substantially greater than the previous campaign, so much so that the new offer could not account for the increase. There were a significant number of inbound calls to the 800 number (about 3% of total response) and about 30% of the lift came from the business reply cards. The custom landing site gave them the greatest lead yield because people could not simply drop the URL extension and enter her site anonymously. In addition, a very big plus came from the deep profile information they gained when people answered the profile questions on the site and from the inbound BRC. This allowed more information to go to the representative. Plus, the inquiry now had a grade.

By letting people have a choice of response portals, the total response always gets a lift. Some inquirers want to respond immediately, so they pick up the phone. They are action people and they want information *now*. Others might not be near a computer, so they fill out the BRC and drop it in the mail. In any event customers want things their way, and it doesn't always include the Internet.

While I served as the VP of Sales for Stac, Inc., a software company, the company president made the statement that the only important source of inquiries for the company was the Web. When I encouraged research to find out the reason why they visited the Web, I found that more than 50% got to the Web from a URL that was in our print advertising. It was interesting, considering the marketing department took the president seriously and was in the process of dramatically reducing print advertising spending. When the print advertisements slowed, so did the Web hits. It took two to four months to reschedule the advertising, and the sales force starved until the lead count (from the print ads *and* the Web) went up again.

It is important to allow the use of as many inquiry entry points as possible so that the prospect will feel free to contact you in the most convenient manner. There are many different points of entry into every company:

1. **Business reply mail (BRM)**

   Also known as a business reply card (BRC), this form of response is very much alive. It is used in direct mail and as a tip-in reply device in print media. And yet, with people's obsession with the Web as the landing site for all inquirers, some companies and their agencies are not using a BRC.

Russell Kern, of Kern Direct and author of the book *S.U.R.E.-Fire Direct Response Marketing*,[1] says,

> The business reply mail (BRM) means of response is not dead. Although it has rivals like the web and toll-free numbers, business reply mail is still a viable response option . . . making it easy for people to respond boosts response rates . . . some responders believe it is easier, simpler, and faster to fill out a reply card than to log onto a web site or call a toll-free number. Give them the BRM option.

When you use a BRM make sure you are asking qualifying questions. Of course, you say, everybody asks questions on a BRC. Not true. Too many BRCs end up in the mailer and only ask for an address without asking four to six questions.

2. **Inbound calls (toll or toll-free).**
   Don't believe that inbound toll-free calls are dead and not used by prospects. If you start placing the 800 number in a prominent position in advertisements or on a BRC or the Web, the calls and hot leads coming into the company will increase. Of course, the Web is the most often-used method of response, but you must allow people to use the response method *they* want to use. While you may only get 3% to 5% of your response from toll-free calls, these are likely to be the most highly qualified, immediate need, hot inquirers. I often hear a company president say, "If they really want our product, they'll pick up the phone and pay for the call themselves." I wondered if these company presidents have forgotten who is selling what and to whom.
   To use your toll-free number effectively, make sure that:

- The toll free number is visible. Don't hide the number in your address block. Make it bold.
- You use the number in the copy and someplace in the advertisement or direct mail piece at least three times.
- You use the word FREE (in all caps) next to the number. Especially with the 866 and other toll-free prefixes, you need the word free next to the number. "Free" is a magnet that draws the eye.

If the inbound calls go to your customer service department, either make sure that operators are trained to handle the call, ask questions, and put the answers in a database or direct the calls to your inside sales department, a telemarketing group that just handles inbound calls, or an outside vendor. Get the toll-free calls handled in a professional manner; after all, these are the hottest inquirers you will probably get for your product or service. Don't disappoint them by letting someone unqualified handle the call or, worse, letting it go to voicemail.

3. **Direct marketing Web landing pages.**
   When using direct mail, it isn't enough to send inquirers to your Web site where they are lost and not counted as inquirers; you should be sending people to campaign-specific landing pages built only for a particular campaign. These landing sites can be simple one-page sites for getting a name and address with a few questions to elaborate sites that can be many layers deep to make good on the registration for offers, presentation of educational materials, and, of course, the obligatory questions.

4. **Coupons in advertisements.**
   Small coupons or reply devices printed on a portion of print media advertisements are still found in many

magazines. You may have to talk your agency into including the coupon on the advertising page since they often complain it ruins their "layout." Even on these small coupons you can fit two to three questions asking about the buyer's intent. Good examples of coupons in advertising can be seen in airline magazine advertising. These advertisements aren't inexpensive, and there are always coupons used by long-term advertisers.

5. **Tip-in reply cards in print magazines.**
Tip-in reply cards are still popular in most magazines. Whether they are bound in or blown in (loose), these cards are used because they work and there is always space on the card for profile questions. While you will often pay a one-page black and white advertising price, experts tell me the use of the card can double and triple responses for an advertisement running next to the card.

6. **Email and Letters.**
Possibly the most neglected of the inquiry sources, emails to the company and even letters often go begging for a response. "Who will answer the email?" is a common plaintive cry from marketing. The answer is that more often than not the email or letter is sent to the inside sales group to follow up. It could go to the telemarketing department for qualification. Many of these are lost as sources to lead-generating campaigns.

7. **Trade show lead retrieval systems/forms.**
Aside from a phone call into the company, trade show inquiries will bring you the most qualified inquiries. A live person has spoken to the inquirer, questions have been asked and answered, and the needs identified. A relationship has been started. The trade show lead form must allow the salesperson who speaks to prospect on the show

floor to completely record the inquirer's needs. The form (or computer screen) should have the four to eight ideal questions you want answered. There should be room for open text comments. Salespeople have to be trained in the use of the forms and why it is important to completely fill out the document.

Unfortunately, hidden within trade show leads are often the most unqualified inquiries that have been created through borrowed interest. The marketing person must be careful to not mix the best and the worst together. Borrowed interest inquiries only stop by the booth for the free pen, T-shirt, to enter a drawing, get the autograph of the celebrity, etc.—nothing more. Show managers, through these offers, use borrowed interest to increase show traffic, but if they don't make an effort to filter out the nonbuyer these unqualified names will pollute what should be your most important lead source. If the person stops by the booth to pick up the promised free item or to enter a drawing, always give them an opportunity to op-out by checking a box that says, "I'm only here for the free gift."

If you have a "show" within the show—presenters or actors doing a live presentation with a theater setup—you can also pollute the outcome by mixing those who want information from you with those who just want to sit down and take a load off or just want to be part of a drawing for a freebie. If you place "forms" on every seat, make sure you allow the person to op-out.

8. **Live seminars.**

This source, possibly as good as trade shows and almost as good as an inbound call, is a great way to find high-quality inquirers. Most often the person has taken time out from their day or evening to show up and listen to your product or educational pitch. The people who register for these events but fail to show are almost as valuable as those that actually attend because you now have their name. For the people at the event, let them opt-out if they are not interested in your products and do not process them as inquiries. You may want to put them into the marketing database to be marketed to in the future, but they don't belong in the database as a sales lead.

9. **Online seminars.**

Online seminars, while used more for education than sales, still find people interested in your products. This group will probably have to be called and mined before you pollute your inquiry database. This inquiry entry point draws many competitors and students. Similar to the live seminar, the online registration list, regardless of attendance, may be almost as good as the people that attend. A direct marketing agency hosted an online seminar that had the usual attendance of about 55% to 60% of the people who registered. Within four months of the program, one of the "no-shows" signed a contract for a substantial ongoing direct marketing program. They subsequently spent in the seven-figure range and created many, many thousands of inquiries for their salespeople and resellers. They may have been a no-show, but they certainly had an interest in the company's products. Not showing doesn't mean they aren't a buyer.

10. **Reader service numbers (RSN) in print advertisements.**

This old-time vehicle is still alive and well. Many print magazines still put reader service numbers on advertisements and press releases. The reply page (some are pre-addressed), normally in the back of the magazine allows you to enter your name and circle the number that corresponds to advertisement. You will get these names electronically or as a printout. The use of the RSN started to fall out of favor during the recession of 1991, when advertising dropped dramatically (and many magazines went out of business). Yet the RSN system is still in use by many magazines. It is better to get a person's name, even without any specific information about buying intent, rather than not get the name at all.

Be cautious about inquiries that come from the magazines that use the RSN for press releases. They may be passing along names from someone who has checked a box that says they are interested in a product category and have not picked you out by name. While it is nice to have these names to market to, sending them to the sales force may contribute to your reputation as a marketer who uses unqualified sales leads.

11. **Representative-entered inquiries.**

Within any response management system you choose, make sure there is an area where the sales representative can enter their own leads. It will be used. Allow room for asking profiles questions and for the sales rep to assign the inquiry to a salesperson or reseller.

12. **Web page contact.**

When I am on a Web site and go to the "Contact Us" section, about 50% of the time I am placed into a simple email response mechanism. At this point I am expected to fill out a blank email, send it to an anonymous someone, who will decide what my needs are and what should be sent as a response. Never mind that the open-text email can't categorize and organize the response in a database. Never mind that the salesperson who will get my request (which may not happen) won't know my time frame for a decision, whether or not I have a budget, whether or not I am the decision-maker, and what I will do with the product (application).

Something triggered a prospect to go to your Web site and ask for information. Don't you want to know the media source that drove him or her to the Web? Without the source information, most marketers attribute the Web as the source of the inquiry when it was most likely some other lead-generating tactic (advertisement, PR release, direct mail, etc.). Some tips about inquiries on the Web:

A. **Don't hide the "Contact Us" button.**

Why do so many companies have the "contact us" link hidden on the bottom of the home page? Ideally, your site should have the contact button appear prominently. It should take the inquirer to a special part of the site and through a series of brief multiple-choice questions.

B. **Ask questions**

The goal is to find out as much as is reasonable about who is inquiring. Questions should be simple multiple choice. Drop-down boxes are ideal because they use little space. If you can get the name and address information and five to six critical, need-to-know questions answered, you'll be successful. You must ask enough questions so that you can grade the inquiry and judge its value. Get only the information you need and don't be greedy. Limit playing the "asterisk game" of having virtually every question mandatory.

Sometimes there is the other extreme: The company will ask 15 to 30 questions, most of which carry an asterisk that threatens to reject your request unless they get the information they want. You have to scroll down several screens to complete the form, and you begin to feel that the company is intrusive and you stop filling out the form. Many of these forms are abandoned before they are completed.

C. The "short, short form" argument!

Some marketers feel you should only ask name and email address on a BRC, on the Web, etc. This way, they contend, the inquirer is not fatigued. The short-form crowd doesn't care where the person heard about you or even their physical address. The address and other information, they believe, will come later if the person is seriously interested in your products.

Unfortunately, marketers using this strategy don't gain much if they don't know who wants information about their products, where in the country or the world they reside, and what their buying intent is. Without this information, the inquirer may make an uninformed choice without the benefit of a salesperson being involved—not a real fine decision.

The short form ends up by adding another time-consuming step to the sales process because someone has to contact the inquirer to find out where they reside and their actual needs. Plus, if you don't have an address, you can't distribute the inquiry to a salesperson.

D. PDF fulfillment (electronic documents).

Consider PDF fulfillment as an alternative to physically fulfilling and mailing literature. While it saves on printed material, handling, and postage, giving people a choice between the electronic version and a mailed version is not only nice but mandatory if you want to be responsive to your prospects' needs. Invented by Adobe Systems and perfected over 15 years, Adobe Portable Document Format (PDF) lets you capture and view robust information—from any application on any computer system—and share it with anyone around the world.

# Capture the Source or Lose ROI

You must know the specific source of every inquiry if you are to know the ROI for your marketing dollars. The inquiry's source is not to be mistaken with its type (PR, direct mail, trade show exhibit, advertisement, radio, DRTV, etc.). If you know the source of the inquiry, which direct mail campaign, which advertisements, etc., you will know the source type. (For instance, sources of inquiries can be:

- A full-page color advertisement in the June 25, 2006 issue of *PC Week*.
- A PR release that appeared in the May 2006 issue of *Clinical Chemistry*.
- A direct mail response from the March 2006 XYZ campaign.
- Trade show leads from Six Sigma at the Sales & Marketing Winter 2006 Conference.

You need this source of information in order to understand where the best leads and sales are.

## *Source or Media Types:*
## *Categories of Primary Inquiry Sources*

Because you have captured the original source of the inquiry, you will now be able to assign the source type to it. These source or media types are as crucial as knowing the specific sources:

- Advertising: print, TV, DRTV, radio.
- Press relations: press releases, press events, press comparisons.
- Trade shows: local, regional, national, and international.
- Direct marketing: mail and outbound telemarketing.
- Seminars: live road shows and online.

You now know that you must have a process to count all inquiries and that you should open up the entry points for inquiries. You must know the source of the inquiry, which will enable you to credit the source type. With these three bits of knowledge you are in a position to create reports to show your results and to control your destiny and the destiny of your company. You will now spend more money on promotions that give you the best return.

## Actions to Take from This Chapter

1. Stop the sales lead leakage. Marketing must hunt down and count every inquiry. They cannot allow inquiries to be lost and data not entered. They must be relentless in their search for 100% of the responses to the campaigns they sponsor.

2. Give the prospect every opportunity to reach you through the most portals of entry into the company. Do not restrict their access to you to just the Web.

3. The source of every inquiry must be recorded. You must know what caused this person to contact you. Was it a referral, a newspaper advertisement, or a direct mail campaign? It's important to know.

4. If you know the source of the inquiry you can name a
   source type category that it belongs to.

## NOTE

[1] Russell M. Kern, *S.U.R.E-Fire Direct Response Marketing* (New York: McGraw Hill, 2001) p. 134.

# 10 Fulfillment, Inquiry Tracking, and Distribution

Most marketers would love to never have to create, print, and mail collateral materials again. That day may come, but for now the printing presses are still humming, and the reported death of printed literature is premature. People still want it.

While company after company has struggled to force buyers to go to the Web for everything, some have found that there are issues with it. What about detailed specifications and "semi-confidential" information? What about color renditions of your products? Not every inquirer's office has a color printer. The reality is that there still is a place for collateral material, maybe in smaller numbers, but still in four color.

The first impression a prospect has of your company is probably through an advertisement that has piqued his or her interest, or it might be a contact with your toll-free phone operator or your Web site. But the first substantive impression a prospect gets of your company is based on the literature you send them. Literature packages of this sort—sent in response to an initial expression of interest—are too often not thought of as part of the "sales" process. Tens of thousands of dollars are spent on printing literature, which is then thrown into a nondescript envelope package accompanied by a poorly written letter, a reply device, and/or information about where the product can be bought.

Thought must go into what you want sent to prospects. Some companies send a single brochure or catalog, but many companies include additional unasked-for pieces of literature. In most cases an ad agency should design the package, which should have a special envelope, a properly written laser-printed letter, and only additional literature that matches the prospect's original request.

If you ask the inquirers, undoubtedly most will say they want it *NOW*, right now, which leans toward the Web as a distribution point. There is no doubt: Print literature use has been reduced as a response vehicle, but it is still being used for response to trade show exhibits, advertisements, and PR, as well as for transmitting semi-confidential information, such as product specifications that companies don't want broadcast on the Web. PDF files are an important method of distributing information, but they shouldn't be relied on exclusively. It's most important to be prepared to give people what they want and how they want it. Give people a chance to request more extensive information through the mail if they wish.

## The Literature Package

Most literature packages will have five elements:

1. The envelope (a flat 9″ × 10″).
2. The letter (personalized laser letter with a signature).
3. The sell piece and product literature.
4. A where-to-buy direction (could be in the letter or a separate office listing).
5. A business reply card (preferably pre-addressed with the prospect's name).

## The Envelope

The envelope should be a flat, large receptacle that will hold everything without folding the contents to get them into the envelope. Don't stuff nicely printed literature into a small 6″ × 9″ envelope. The outside of the envelope should have the words:

"You requested this literature"

This forethought solves several issues:

- The mail room or the gatekeeper will not throw it out.
- The recipient will be reminded that they asked for the literature.

## The Letter

The letter is definitely a sales piece. You should use the same care in its creation that you would use for a letter in a direct mail piece. Have your agency write the letter or better yet have them design the entire response package. The letter should be:

- Dated.
- Personally addressed.
- Preferably one page (this isn't a direct mail package).
- Refer to their inquiry and the product inquired about.
- Tell a story. Speak to the inquirer about the benefits of your company in human, down-to-earth language that the inquirer can identify with. Use a dull product pitch, and it will go unread. Tell a story, and you may capture their imagination.
- Be signed by someone in sales, preferably the salesperson who will be calling on them.
- Below the postscript some companies will list the names of

the closest resellers or the sales office if not the office of the person signing the letter.

• Make sure that the postscript sells.

Some companies will replace the letter with a tent card that says: "Thanks for the inquiry. Call us if you need anything." Sometimes the tent card is quite large and is a non-laser printed form letter. Advice: Tent cards tend to go unread.

## The Literature

The literature itself should be what the person asked for and nothing more. I often hear a product manager say, "Well, while we're sending them this piece of literature, let's send them these three multiple-page brochures, a catalog, a PR release, and a few specifications sheets. Maybe they'll get excited about these other products." When the recipient gets the multipound literature package with so much unasked-for material, their first inclination is to set it aside until he or she has more time to look through it. Will this ever happen? Probably not in their lifetime. After a while, the monster package is most likely edged off the desk and into the trash.

The other obvious reason to send people only what they asked for is cost. Put one four-color, four-page brochure in the package with a letter, and it might cost $1 in labor, a few cents for the letter, and $2 for the brochure and postage. Add the second unasked-for brochure, and you've doubled the cost of the contents and, probably, the postage. The cost of the literature package can zoom from a few dollars to $10 to $20 or more. This is a tactical mistake that can cost the company tens of thousands of dollars over a period of time.

## Where to Buy and the BRC

The where-to-buy instruction in the literature package is crucial to creating a preference. If the sale will be made by your salesperson, have them sign the letter. If you are referring the inquirer to a reseller or retail store, give them the name(s) of the closest place to find the product, but sign the letter from the highest sales executive in the company.

The last piece in the package is the business reply card. If you want to make your pitch for other products, this is the place to do it. If the BRC is pre-addressed with the prospect's name, etc., you will get a higher percentage back than if it is not pre-addressed. This may not be easy for you to do if the fulfillment is handled in-house, but it is easy if done with an outside vendor.

## Common Mistakes in Fulfillment Packages

The most common mistakes in literature packages are:

1. The literature arrives too late. I was at a home improvement show last year and asked for literature from about 50 companies. The average response time was about three weeks. Only a few took the time to send out what I asked for within a day or so. Some companies took six months or longer to send me what I requested. Send literature within three days of the show's end. No exceptions.

2. The company does not put a statement on the envelope that says, "This is the literature you requested" or some such statement.

3. The company sends non-requested literature.

4. They send photocopied literature.

5. There is no sales letter inside the package.

6. The letter is there, but it is poorly written and doesn't sell. It is often photocopied.

7. Large-format brochures that should not be folded are stuffed into a number 10 or a 6″ × 9″ envelope.

8. There isn't any information about where to buy the

product—no list of dealers or representatives or an enclosed business card.

9. There isn't a business reply card in the package. It isn't unusual that a package of literature is stored for future viewing. If there is a business reply card in the package, it will be used about 2% to 5% of the time at a later date.

## Don't Send Literature to Competitors

It doesn't make economic senses to send literature to a competitor. Your company can spend thousands of dollars being nice to someone who is trying to take your business away. Make it difficult for competitors to get your literature. If they are determined, they will get something from someone, but it may not be in time for the sales pitch they have to make to others or the engineering project they are working on. Have your inquiry-management system screen the names of competing companies. Why spend money on a competitor and make it easy to take away your customers?

I know a very small company that developed a composite product for use in high-stress situations in research. This product was lighter in weight than competitors' products, all of which were made of special steel alloys, and appeared to outperform even the largest competitor's products.

The product was introduced at a major show. The crowds at the company's little 10-foot booth were amazing. It was also amazing if any buyers could get through all of the competitors who were lined up in front of the booth. On the first day of the show the largest competitor politely asked if they could take some literature. The company president said sure, why not. Within minutes the literature was faxed to the home office and was shown at an emergency engineering and marketing meeting that was called within hours of the show's opening.

By noon of the second day new literature refuting the claims made by the small upstart was on display at the large competitor's booth. After all, the upstart was challenging all of the hitherto known norms of a $500 million market. At this point the large competitor is still in business. I understand they are selling one product that is not unlike what the small upstart was showing. The upstart is no longer in business.

Screening for competitors isn't easy. You have to put in all possible names and acronyms. You might also want to screen for the names of competitors' executives. To do it right you may have to visually look at every inquiry. Most vendors do this for you automatically.

## Duplicate Inquiries

You need a business rule for identifying and handling duplicates. If someone has inquired during the last month and a second request comes in, what should you do? Did the inquirer request information on the same product? If not, it isn't a duplicate. Considering that people often just make a second call to a general toll-free number rather than to the specific rep to request the same literature, you can get a duplicate. The question is did you follow up on the person the first time they inquired? Mixed responses come from this sort of direct question. Sometimes a salesperson will call once, but then give up without following through. If the sales rep leaves a voicemail but doesn't make a second call, the inquirer might call again.

In one instance, a company was slow to get literature sent and the sales reps were equally slow in calling the prospect. It turned out many of the suspects were calling in a second time to get the literature they asked for and they really wanted a salesperson to call them. The second call was costly to take, costly to put through the system, and it skewed the response numbers until someone saw that the duplication rate was into double digits.

In my experience, only about 2% to 3% of the inquiries are genuine duplicates. While not an insignificant number, it isn't unusual that an inquirer will forget who they inquired from while on their search for a product.

## Tracing Inquiries from the Same Company: Historic Trace

It isn't unusual that several people from the same company will inquire about your products and services. They might be co-owners or members of a buying committee. Two typical examples are several doctors in a group practice or several engineers working on the same project. It's essential to know who the people are, the products of interest, and the disposition of the inquiry. These inquiries are usually not thought of as duplicates because they are from a different person and often for different products. Just because the company name and address are the same, it isn't necessarily a duplicate.

If you are managing inquiries in-house or going to a vendor (software or service), make sure that the system enables the salesperson to trace these kinds of inquiries and connect them. When a salesperson gets an inquiry and initially reviews it, if there are one or even a dozen records flagged as being from the same company, it will remind him or her of previous sales, lost sales, or even ongoing sales situations (other sales reps or resellers). Tracking can connect the people and products and provides a history of a previous relationship.

Building a history of your relationship with a prospect's company is important and having a salesperson who is aware of all of the previous contact, sales, and even losses is also important. Tracing previous inquirers, regardless of final disposition, should be an important part of every inquiry-management system.

# Distributing Inquiries to Sales Territories

When companies have complicated distribution channels, who should get the lead? The answer is always the same: Inquiries should be sent by the most direct route to the person who has the final face-to-face sales authority.

If it is true that nothing happens until the sale is made, it is just as true that the sale can't be made unless you can put the right salesperson together with the prospect. How this is done and the instructions or business rules given to the salesperson who must make contact is crucial to your company's success. Inquiries and leads shouldn't go into a black hole or a salesperson's trunk, email box, or contact management system without some resolution. While salespeople may be comfortable in hiding the final disposition of an inquiry, you want to know because you've probably spent from $50 to $1,000 to find the potential buyer.

Assuming that you have qualified the inquiry in some manner, you have the simple task of sending it to the right person. You can distribute the inquiry by:

1. **Zip codes.**
   Still the ideal way to create territories if you have hard-coded sales territories and your sales force is not large (under 200).

2. **Longitude/latitude.**
   Ideal for large distribution channels that do not have hard-coded, dedicated sales territories. This method is best for consumer products whereby the end user asks where the product can be purchased and you tell them that they have several choices: One reseller is 5.5 miles from them, one is 10 miles, and one is 12 miles. Some computer programs will review the inquirer's address and, using longitude and

latitude, pick out the nearest resellers and present them in a file so they can be printed on a letter.

### 3. Rotating.

The computer system can rotate the reseller names within a zip code so one name doesn't come up first all of the time for a certain area.

### 4. US counties.

Not as popular a system as it was in the past. Dividing territories by counties is similar to an area code. Counties stretch across geographic barriers such as rivers, mountains, deserts, and vast open spaces.

### 5. Telephone area code.

Area codes are a good separator of territories if you have inside salespeople. With inside salespeople you aren't worried about geographic barriers within an area code, which can make life difficult for outside salespeople.

### 6. Geographic boundaries.

Area codes, zip codes, or longitude/latitude can be aided by geographic boundaries. Geographic distribution lines are often drawn by mountain ranges, rivers, state lines, and even streets in major cities. For example, territory X gets the area north of Belmont Ave and east of Mannheim Road to the lake shore, while territory Y gets south of Belmont to Cermak Road and from the lake to Mannheim.

### 7. Product.

Low-value commodity products are often sent to inside sales reps or resellers because outside people can't afford to call on accounts with a low dollar value. High-value products are often sent to direct salespeople or to VARs (value added resellers), or consultative salespeople inside or outside of your organization. The main thing is you have to be able to sort by product, value, etc., in order to know who you will be sending the inquiries and leads to. The more sophisticated the computer program or service, the more likely you'll be able to sort by product and/or value and other variables.

8. **National accounts.**
Virtually every company today has some sort of national accounts program for its best customers. Whether it is a large buying group for hospitals or a computer company's users group, companies understand the need for special purchasing circumstances for large buyers. Your inquiry-management system should be able to recognize the name of a buying group or company and divert that inquiry to the national account manager handling it.

9. **Grandfathered accounts.**
Grandfathered accounts are labeled as such because they are historically reserved for a salesperson who has earned the right to exclusively call on a customer. Very often the salesperson serving this account will cross territory lines. Sometimes a salesperson will be assigned a new sales territory and an account will go with them. Similar to national accounts, your inquiry-management system should be able to recognize the account names and properly assign them.

# Sending Inquiries and Leads to Direct Salespeople

Direct salespeople, employees of the company, will often get inquiries distributed by zip codes, product value, etc. Send the inquiry out imbedded in an email and you won't hear much from them. Send inquiries and leads to the salesperson in a spreadsheet, and you may receive a resolution report. Dump all inquiries (regardless of qualification) into your contact management program or CRM system, and you will get reports following the business rules you have established for the reps and your ability to pull their reports off the system. You will also get a bloated database of unqualified suspects.

If the sales force does not have an SFA or CRM system, the inquiry is sent by email or via a secure Web site to the direct salesperson. The rep reads about the inquirer in the email or clicks on the link within the email and is sent to a secure, password-protected site that contains the salesperson's leads. From this point they "work" the inquiry over time until there is some resolution.

Very few outside vendors or companies pass inquiries along to salespeople by snail mail or by fax. Ease of use has to be the determining factor for not just lead distribution but also in getting the resolution. Salespeople need the prospect's name as soon as possible, and marketing wants to know how valid the inquiry source was so they can stop spending money on things that don't work and spend more on things that do work.

Reseller networks will often get the inquiries on spreadsheets and through email because they are not invited to be a part of the company's CRM or contact management team. This is a mistake. These resellers should be held no less accountable for the leads given to them than the direct salespeople. If resellers are encouraged or "invited" to report on the results of an inquiry, they will do so to the same degree or higher than the company's own direct salespeople.

## The Importance of Getting There First

Showing up first is important to you and to the prospect. Taking their phone call without delay, fulfilling the requested literature within a few days and not months, having a salesperson call in a timely manner and not giving up too soon, are the marks of a professional company that takes its prospects and eventually it's customers seriously. Good service before the sale is an indication of the service that will be rendered after the sale.

## Actions to Take from This Chapter

1. Get the information into the suspects' hands as soon as humanly possible. Whether by mail or a PDF file, be quick.
2. Make sure that the literature package is professionally presented. No photocopied literature, small envelopes, or more than what was asked for.
3. The letter should be laser printed and it should sell.
4. Avoid the common mistakes for literature packages.
5. Do not send literature to competitors.
6. Carefully screen for duplicates.
7. Show previous inquirers: historic trace.
8. Distribute inquiries to people who have the responsibility to give you the resolution.

# 11 Closing the Inquiry Loop

As much as we are weary of the phase, "closing the loop," it still is the best description of what passes for accountability in sales and marketing. I discussed the 100% Follow-up Rule in Chapter 4 and elsewhere, but how does it get done? Exactly what is the loop? Who closes it and why does anyone care?

*Closed loop reporting* means that a sales representative has given management a final resolution for every inquiry. This doesn't mean only the ones that are geographically close, or the ones with phone numbers, or the ones with answers to profile questions. This means 100% of all inquiries.

Along with a business rule that says that sales reps must follow up 100%, they must record the resolution of the inquiry. If you tell reps you want resolution within 90 days, they will close out the inquiry prior to a final sales resolution and you won't know what happened to 75% of the inquiries over the rest of their life cycle. For closure the salespeople need final disposition categories with specific resolution names and codes. AdTrack Corporation calls them Sales Action Taken (SAT) codes, which is an appropriate name.

Resolution codes are not to be confused with marketing and sales stages. Marketing and sales stages are the progressive steps that a sales inquiry passes through until it is finally resolved. As the inquiry gets boosted from suspect to prospect, etc., it may die and a final resolution must be entered. Common sales resolution codes[1] are:

1. Sold/Sold for the company. When an inquiry has a grade of sold, there should be a place to enter the final product sold (it could be different from the original inquiry) and the dollars.
2. Bought other. While no one likes bad news, hearing that a sale has been lost at least tells management who it was lost to and the dollars lost.
3. Not qualified. Every salesperson gets inquiries from people who are not qualified to buy. They may have wanted something bigger, smaller, lighter, a different color, or a lower price. This is where competitive inquirers are placed.
4. Could not contact. Some people are simply unreachable. As I mentioned earlier, after five attempts it is a game of diminishing returns to reach an inquirer.
5. No interest. Similar to Category 3, but this category can contain consultants, the press, and academics.
6. Info only. This inquirer is often a student, but it can also be people (engineers) who say they just wanted information for a file. Maybe a far distant use.
7. Future remarket. Not everyone wants to buy right away, and their need may be far into the future. They often say their inquiry is for information only but please stay in touch. These people are ideal for marketing to remarket to until the person inquires again. When people say they will buy far into the future, they may also be lying.
8. Future. It is into this category that a sales rep places an inquiry that is not yet dead and may have some future inter-

est. This is a parking place where reps hide those that they don't want to give up on.

Regardless of the categories (eight to ten is typical), make sure the names mean something to you. Reports will show which inquiry sources (trade shows, magazines, direct mail, etc.) are giving you the greatest number of unusable categories. These are the inquiry sources you probably will want to avoid in the future.

## Giving Salespeople Reasons to Comply

Salespeople, like all of us, determine what is nice and what is necessary to do their jobs. If they are not given enough good reasons and adequate "incentives" for following up sales inquiries, they will follow-up only on those that they feel are worth their effort. John Wanamaker, the industrialist (1838 –1922), was famous for saying that, "Half the money I spend on advertising is wasted; the trouble is I don't know which half." The same principle is true for sales inquiry follow-up: Unless a salesperson actually calls and speaks to every inquirer, they can't tell which one is good and which one isn't.

As discussed in Chapter 2, if you want to get follow-up, simply make it a business rule. Create the rule, enforce it, and everything will be fine. Right? Maybe. Unsubstantiated or unexplained rules are usually considered to be optional by salespeople. Free will and lax sales management encourages them to make their own choices on the value of what corporate is creating for them. As long as they get the sale, they figure, no one will bother them. It isn't enough to tell salespeople what you want done. You must tell them *why* you want it done.

And the best reasons appeal to their self-interest.

# Seven Ways to Motivate Salespeople to Follow up Inquiries

1. **Greed: They will make more money.**
   Talk to more people and they will sell more product. It is a simple law of averages.

2. **Fear: They must make quota.**
   Sometimes sales reps need to be reminded that a sales quota is a contract between the salesperson and the company. In order to make quota, they must sell product at a predictable level, which can only be done if they speak to more people than the number of customers who must be converted every year. A constant flow of new prospects helps them do this.

3. **More fear: It's a condition of employment.**
   The only certain way a salesperson will understand and comply with your 100% follow-up rule is if the rule is a condition of employment. It should be stated in the job description that each salesperson reads and signs upon joining the sales department. While all of the reasons cited here are important, this is the reason that they most often respond to.

4. **Guilt: Inquiries are expensive.**
   Salespeople must be told that each inquiry costs the company $50 to $1,000. If they only follow up 50%, they are wasting 50% of the company's money being spent on their behalf.

5. **More guilt: They will disappoint potential customers.**
   The suspect who has contacted the company expects to be contacted. The first test of a company's responsiveness to a potential customer's needs is to ask for information and

get it (either from the literature or a personal contact from a salesperson). If the salesperson doesn't follow up 100%, those inquirers not followed up will be disappointed in the company and the company's brand name (and, ultimately, the individual sales rep) will suffer. Remember the last time you got bad service at a restaurant? Afterward, did you say the waitress was to blame or did you blame the restaurant? Probably both, but the restaurant's name definitely comes up.

6. **Exclusivity: Only the salesperson can close out the inquiry.**
   No one in the company except the sales representative can accurately report back on the inquiry resolution. With all of the effort and money being spent to find the prospect, the success or failure of marketing hinges on the inquiry resolution from each salesperson. Only the salespeople's accumulated opinions for each inquiry, when added together and judged by source, will tell management if the money they spent on marketing was successful. That is a lot of responsibility.

7. **Deliverance: Now marketing will stop asking.**
   If they close out the inquiries, everyone will stop bothering them.

Five things happen when salespeople comply with the 100% Follow-up Rule:

1. Reported follow-up increases from 20% to 70% compliance at any point in time (the other 30% of the inquiries are being worked).
2. Sales increase in pace with the follow-up of the inquiries (90 to 180-day lag as conversion goes up with follow-up).
3. Salespeople sell more and make quota more often.

4. Marketing spending shifts to the lead-generation tactics that are most successful.

5. Sales management is in better control as they can compare a salesperson's follow-up of the inquiry (including speed of follow-up), the aging of the inquiry, and the salesperson's disposition of it.

Of course the system must be easy to use, but, even disregarding that, salespeople will comply if you give them enough good reasons. Contrary to popular belief, salespeople like discipline. Their whole business life is guided by strict guidelines of what they can do and what they cannot do. The most successful salespeople are highly disciplined.

## Reseller Compliance

What about resellers, dealers, and the like? Even very large channels of distribution, with more than 1,000 resellers, will comply with a 70% to 85% compliance rate. Just because they are independent sales channels doesn't mean they don't want inquiries and won't comply with your rules if you give them the inquiry and otherwise deal with them reasonably.

Resellers like getting inquiries, but without training, an easy-to-use system of lead retrieval, and sensible business rules to guide them, they will not "close the loop" as you request. The reasons have to do with independence, fear of sharing information, and the difficulty in communicating. Unfortunately, most companies present the inquiry to the reseller in such an awkward manner (email, spreadsheets, paper) that communicating the disposition becomes difficult and time consuming.

Often the reseller is excluded from the company's lead-reporting system (sales force automation/contact management/CRM system). This promotes two classes of salespeople: (1) company salespeople with their computer fully tied into the company's CRM system and (2) the reseller, who gets his leads by email and spreadsheet with an impersonal order, "Tell us what happens to these inquiries, or else." This simply creates an "us-them" relationship that is not conducive to cooperation.

Many companies have decided that if they cannot let the reseller into their "inside" system for lead distribution and follow-up, they will find an outsourced system that is as good as their own but runs independently of the company's CRM system. Ad-Track Corporation, one of several such service companies and an ASP model software provider, has found that many companies will use their system for lead distribution and resolution for both the corporate sales staff and resellers at the front end of the customer acquisition cycle. This allows a separation of the databases. The result is that resellers have an easy-to-use system to complete the sales cycle and the corporation's salespeople can transfer the sold prospect over to the corporate CRM system. The AdTrack system allows an inquiry to be placed before resellers; if it is not opened and worked, it will be pulled back and redistributed to someone who cares.

They are not alone in using this push-and-pull model. Another company that provides a stand-alone software package to perform this same function for sales channel management is BlueRoads.[2] Their program can not only give the sales channel person a lead, but it automatically takes it away if the person doesn't comply with specific rules and makes it available of another reseller. BlueRoads says that, "It is estimated that fewer than 40% of the leads a vendor distributes to its channel partners are actually contacted in a timely manner."[3] Regardless of how you solve this issue of reseller compliance, the linchpin is always ease of use: Make it easy, and it is much more likely that they will live with your business rule.

## Making It Easy to Report: Compliance, the Key to Success

The reason most salespeople don't comply with follow-up rules is that it is difficult to report to marketing on the resolution of the inquiry. It gets back to how the inquiry was given to them. If the inquiry is mailed to them, they have to keep a copy for themselves and mark a resolution on another copy and mail it back. If it is faxed, same routine. If you send the inquiry to the salesperson via email, they are often asked to respond by email or on a spreadsheet. None of these methods is easy for the salesperson or the marketing department. This kind of reporting eats up large portions of the salespeople's valuable sales time.

If the salesperson returns a spreadsheet with the resolutions to sales and marketing management, someone has to read it, go back to the inquiry database wherever it resides, and manually enter the code into the database. Just about now someone reading this is asking, "Who is using paper leads, faxes, or even spreadsheets to distribute leads?" The answer is more companies than you would imagine. That's the point: Lead distribution using these methods will never give you the results you want or a resolution that can be measured.

Of course, many companies are using an in-house software program to manage the inquiries, a sales force automation program that also presents inquiries, or a vendor that manages the whole inquiry process and uses an application service provider interface to deliver the inquiries. Regardless of what you use, if you do not make it easy for the salesperson to tell you what happened to the inquiry, your whole program will be in jeopardy. Salespeople have enough to contend with today with the different systems for order entry, order retrieval, quoting, contact management, lost sales reports, pipeline forecasting reports, customer relationship management system (which may or may not do all of the above), lead retrieval and reporting, etc., etc., ad nauseam. Just learning and keeping up with the information access side of their jobs isn't easy. I have seldom given a workshop or seminar without someone from an SFA or CRM company wildly waving their raised hands while saying, "We can do all of that, we can do it all, every last bit and byte in our system."

That's a fine statement, but before you force the salespeople to use an inquiry management reporting system, make sure real salespeople test it. Make sure it is easy for the salespeople to use right out of the box or don't do it.

## Actions to Take from This Chapter

1. Create sales resolution codes that make sense for your company, your salespeople, and your marketplace.
2. Tell your salespeople why 100% follow-up benefits them and you. Use my seven reasons or better yet create your own. It doesn't hurt to stress to them that it is a condition of employment.
3. The system of compliance and reporting must be easy to use.

### NOTES

[1] Codes as used by AdTrack Corporation, Cedar Rapids, Iowa. Other companies use similar terms.

[2] BlueRoads, San Mateo, CA; www.blueroads.com.

[3] BlueRoads White Paper: "Best Practices in Lead Management," 2003, page 2.

# Estimating the Number of Inquiries Needed and Finding Hot Sources

# 12 Estimating How Many Inquiries Is Enough

Marketers suspect that they should know the quotas for the company's sales channels, but the great majority doesn't. What good does it do if you go to trade shows, place print media advertisements, use online advertisements, use direct mail and PR to create demand without knowing how much has to be sold? Unfortunately, the majority of companies create a marketing budget based on last year's budget with no regard to tying the demand creation spending to the need for inquiries based on the sales force's need to sell a specific amount of product in a specific time frame.

## Too Little, Too Much, Or Just Right?

The question is, how does a marketer know exactly how many inquiries to create and how much to spend? While estimating is not an exact science, you can come fairly close to predicting the number of inquiries needed to make quota, and after a little practice you can become quite good at creating demand based on need (quota), not on an obscure budget percentage from last year.

Claude Hopkins, in his book *Scientific Advertising*, published in 1923, said, "Advertising is salesmanship . . . The only purpose of advertising is to make sales. It is profitable or unprofitable according to its actual sales."[1] And 83 years later, Sergio Zyman in an article on Better Management.com said, "Advertising has one job, to get more people to buy more of what is being advertised. Without demanding that your advertising first generate results, all you may be doing is allowing your agency to artistically enjoy themselves at your expense."[2]

It all starts with the sales goals for the company. Imagine that your company needs $10 million in new sales and the product is priced at $10,000, with a market share of 25%. Your steps are:

1. **How much will you sell without lead-generating activities?**
   Estimate how much you will sell with the momentum you have (current pipeline velocity) without any lead generation activity. Assume that this is $5 million. This is your baseline.

2. **Marketing must create demand to fill the rest of the expected growth.**
   You now know that your promotions will have to help the sales force close another $5 million. If the total market needed to get $10 million growth is available and your sales force has the time and can service the number of inquiries that you will produce, you now have to find the magic number of inquiries required to make quota. The formula is:

   Sales goal / average sales price / 45% / market share percent = inquiries needed

   We therefore have:

   $5,000,000 / $10,000 / 45% / 25% = 4,444 inquiries.

## The Good News: A One-Year-Lead Generation Plan Gives You Sales for 18 to 20 months

If 100% of the inquiries are followed up and all the buyers are contacted, the 4,444 inquiries will have a yield of $5 million. But there is a caveat within this projection: We must assume that the company will generate these inquiries over a full year (inquiries and leads flowing in each month). This means about 370 inquiries per month. Because it takes a full year from a particular month's inquiries to reach full maturation (45% turn into a sale from someone and you get your market share), you can see that inquiries generated in Q2 of a year will give you sales in Q1 of the *following year*. Inquiries generated in Q3 will give you sales through Q2 of the *following year*, and so on.

The inquiries from these months and quarters generate immediate sales in this year but also sales in the following year. This is your sales pipeline. The good news is that a one-year promotional plan will generate sales for three quarters into the following year. The bad news is that you must pump up inquiries so that you'll make the $5 million forecast for *this year*. The need, therefore, is to generate enough inquiries to make this year's numbers, and to do that you must create 60% more inquiries than originally forecast.

## The 60% Factor: Marketing Pipeline

The 60% factor means you must generate 60% more inquiries to offset the long-term buyers that will not make a decision until sometime in the following year. You can call this building a marketing pipeline of inquiries to supply the sales pipeline. It is similar to building an inventory of finished goods that must remain on the shelf until used.

Exhibits 12.1 and 12.2 demonstrate how this works.

The example in Exhibit 12.1 shows a continuous lead

# EXHIBIT 12.1
## Lead Generation Momentum

| | First Year | | | | Second Year | | | Total |
|---|---|---|---|---|---|---|---|---|
| | Q1 | Q2 | Q3 | Q4 | Q1 | Q2 | Q3 | |
| Inquiries Per Quarter | 1778 | 1778 | 1778 | 1778 | | | | 7112 |
| Sales Per Quarter | 50 | 100 | 150 | 200 | 150 | 100 | 50 | 800 |
| Average Sale Price | 10,000 | 10,000 | 10,000 | 10,000 | 10,000 | 10,000 | 10,000 | |
| Market Share | 25% | 25% | 25% | 25% | 25% | 25% | 25% | |
| Qualified Lead Ratio | 45% | 45% | 45% | 45% | 45% | 45% | 45% | |
| Sales Results | 500,000 | 1,000,000 | 1,500,000 | 2,000,000 | 1,500,000 | 1,000,000 | 500,000 | 8,000,000 |

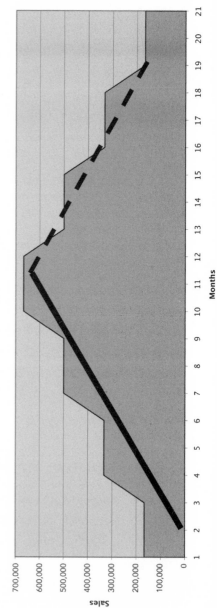

Sales build quarter by quarter and when leads stop in Q4 of year one sales continue but decline.

generation momentum of 1,778 inquiries per quarter or 593 a month. Exhibit 12.1 graphs the sales ramp. In this example inquiries come in steadily over the 12-month period, building quarter by quarter, and then stops. And yet revenue continues to come in over the following three quarters. For illustration purposes this assumes lead generation stops in month 13, but the revenue continues.

Exhibit 12.1 shows how sales from inquiries increase quarter by quarter and then in Q1 of year two sales decline as the inquiries already in the system begin to run their course. If inquiries are generated in Q1 of year two, sales will be supported and the decline will not happen. Therefore, in order to create sales of $5 million in Year One with an integrated plan to bring in a continuous flow of inquiries over the full year, you will have to generate not 4,444 inquiries but closer to 7,100. This will give you a yield of $5 million in sales in the current year and another $3 million for the pipeline for the following year. Of course, this assumes that you have 100% follow-up. This is the pipeline just from inquiries. Salespeople have a pipeline from their own efforts, previous inquiries, cold calling and customers, etc., which makes up the rest of the momentum needed to make whatever growth is expected in the following year.

Thus:

1. **Predict.** You can predict the number of inquiries needed to help your salespeople make quota.
2. **Create enough demand.** Because your promotional plan of lead generation continues all year, you must use the 60% factor (hedge) to be sure you are generating enough demand.
3. **Hedge.** The 60% hedge generates income into Q1 through Q3 of the following year.
4. **Measure results and adjust.** To do this right, you have to

start with the basic formula: Assume that you will generate more inquiries than are needed by the sales channel, and adjust as you go. If the market share percent that you used is too high, you'll know it within one sales cycle if you don't make the sales goal based on this market share number. The sales cycle is the time it takes to close an average sale. If you have guessed the market share percent too low and are closing more sales than expected, you will be confronted with the greed question:

> Should you then back off of spending on marketing because the closing ratio is higher than expected and you don't need as many inquiries as you projected, or continue spending because the money is in the budget?

Most companies will slam their foot on the gas pedal and continue spending and driving sales.

## Why One Source of Inquiries Isn't Enough

"How is business?" the consultant asked the marketing manager of the Fortune 500 company, a medical devices manufacturer. "Business," he said, "is going OK I guess, but we are a bit behind forecast, and while we're still leaders, the competition is nipping at our heels and causing problems." This was the situation:

The company is selling a medical device to hospitals (price: $100,000+). Using print advertising and some trade shows, they had generated 600 inquiries for their salespeople in the current year. The total number of devices sold into hospitals every year was 1,500 units. Each unit had a yearly supply requirement of at least as much, if not twice the value, of the instrument cost. They sold an annual total of 700 units. The numbers worked out this way:

- Total available market: 1500 instruments sold
- Company sold: 700 instruments
- Competition sold: 800 instruments
- The company only created 600 inquiries of which there were 270 actual buyers
- Instrument sales found by marketing: 124

When the numbers are written out, a couple of things pop out:

1. Sales found 576 buyers on their own (700-124) from previous inquirers in the pipeline, etc.
2. Marketing found 124 buyers within the 270 (45% of 600 inquiries).
3. There were 1,230 buyers in the marketplace not identified by marketing, and sales closed 576 units on their own.
4. However, sales lost 800 sales, which they may or may not have known about.

The salespeople probably were aware of many of the other 800 units being sold. But because the salespeople had to find these opportunities on their own and because marketing knew nothing about them, some thoughts emerge:

- Regardless of how good a salesperson is, he or she will not likely know of all opportunities that surface. Hospitals with competitive products due for replacement may not invite in all manufacturers.
- To truly compete in the other opportunities salespeople would have had to spend hours of valuable time to find (cold calls) the hospitals.
- It would have been better if marketing could have found 100% of the available buyers, or at least 75% to 80% and passed them on to sales.
- What would have happened had marketing generated

1,200 to 1,500 inquiries instead of only 600? Would sales have closed more? Of course.

- Could they get the added 1,200 inquiries from just advertising and exhibits? Highly unlikely or it would have happened. They will have to be more aggressive with other potential lead-generating tactics (PR, direct mail, online advertising, search engine optimization, online or live seminars).

It is typical that 50% to 75% of a company's sales still come from opportunities found by the salespeople with little or no help from marketing. And yet does that make economic sense? If marketing sets as a goal to find all the available opportunities and help nurse prospects, and track them and source them to ads, shows, direct mail, etc., wouldn't the company's cost of sales decrease and it sales increase? In short, if salespeople spend more time in face-to-face selling rather than cold calling and knocking on doors, the cost of sales will go down and sales revenue go up (the reason given for nurturing).

This manager looked at the numbers and decided to do something about it. In the next year he was not able to increase the inquiry count by 100%, but he did push it up by 60%. He sent direct mail, increased outbound lead generation calling, pumped up the PR, set higher goals at trade shows (trained the salespeople how to sell at shows) and several things happened: Sales increased. Quotas were met. Competitors were taken down a few notches.

When it comes to promoting their products, some people have very strong opinions—and it is the opinions that get in the way. Some believe in the Web, others in just direct mail. Most will agree to go to trade shows, but not all think Web-hosted seminars are worth it. Media advertising (print and online) is thought by many to be the basis for most marketing programs as well as PR (after all some say, its free), but not all think that live road show seminars are worth the time and effort. So, what really works? Where should a marketing manager put her money to find the most buyers?

The answer is you will seldom find one source of promotion that will find all of the available buyers for your products. Doctors don't read just one publication. IT managers don't just use the Web to buy computers and servers. Purchasing people don't scan PR releases for new products they can buy. Buyers, unfortunately, don't huddle in one corner where they can be easily identified. Buyers hide. Buyers lie. Buyers are evasive and conceal themselves in nooks and crannies of the marketplace; in order to find them you have to be smart, sneaky, and persistent. You have to set a goal to find all of the available buyers or at least as many buyers as you can afford to find.

Companies hire salespeople to find buyers and to sell. Unfortunately, most salespeople have quotas far above their abilities to personally seek out and touch every potential buyer in their territory; they need help. Of course, you can expect that more than 50% of the sales they make will come from personal sales efforts and existing customers, but true market gains have to come from promotional programs that reach out into the marketplace, where the buyers are hiding, and lure them out into the open. You can't do this by using just advertising, or only hosting a Web site, or sending out one direct mail piece. You need multiple promotions from multiple sources to expose your message through all communications channels. Here's how you do it if you want to gain market share at an extraordinary rate.

## Gaining Market Share at an Extraordinary and Predictable Rate

First, determine the size of the total available marketplace. If you are selling a high-speed printer and research reports indicate that

12,000 of these devices are sold each year, you now know the size of the playing field. This is the Total Available Marketplace (TAM).

However, you might not serve the Total Available Marketplace because of your product's size, features, price, etc.

For instance, let's assume that there are several versions of this product. One version is a high-speed model and a second is a slightly slower version. The Total Available Market is about 12,000 printers per year, but the Servable Available Market (SAM) for this company is about 6,000 units.

Marketing's job is to find the most likely buyers for these 6,000 units. Out of the 300,000 businesses that could buy a product such as this, marketing must choose those most likely to buy this more advanced, expensive version. The final number of businesses might be winnowed down to about 125,000. A reasonable guess is that somewhere among these 125,000 businesses are 6,000 who are going to make a decision to buy a $3,000 product. The marketplace is $18 million dollars for this category of printers. Now the challenge is to choose the most economical promotional vehicles to reach them.

Direct mail is usually an easy option, so marketing can try it. But not all mail is opened (the average percentage for opened mail is 45%). So these are the facts of the situation:

- Total Available Market (TAM) in units   12,000
- Servable Available Market (SAM)          6,000
- 250 units sold per month on average
   —Total number of businesses                         300,000
   —Total businesses that are likely to buy            125,000

If the company has used just media advertising in the past, it might want to use other forms of promotion to reach all of the available buyers. It seems that print and online media can't find enough inquiries.

The challenge here is to use other lead generation vehicles to reach as much of the available market as possible in any given month. Marketing can add some brand advertising to the mix, spotted with periodic press releases on new printers. Marketing can schedule trade shows and online live events. The need is consistent sales and that can only be achieved by creating consistent demand. The new promotional program is shown below. Note the sales lead projection.

Integrated Marketing Communications uses multiple communications tactics to find the maximum total available buyers. In the six-month example in Exhibit 12.2 note that inquiries generally increase from month to month, quarter over quarter, keeping pace with the probable quota demand.

Notice that the integrated communications plan brings in inquiries from many sources; there is an average inquiry count per month. From one quarter to the next there is an increase in inquiries (in sync with quota increases). There is even an estimate of the inquiries per month per representative on average.

Pump this kind of consistent lead generation program into an inquiry management process with the 100% follow-up rule and watch sales increase.

The increase in inquiries in Exhibit 12.2 should progress month by month in step with the quotas demands.

When I speak on this subject and talk about the common sense of connecting quota expectations to marketing demand creation I am seeing greater acceptance. In any given group about 30% say they are connecting the dots between quotas and inquiries created and eventually ROI. It is being done.

## Actions to Take from This Chapter

1. Everyone that touches the customer and influences the sale in any manner must know the quotas that the company

# EXHIBIT 12.2
## Integrated Lead Generation Campaign Q1 & Q2

| | January | February | March | April | May | June |
|---|---|---|---|---|---|---|
| **Print Ads** | | | | | | |
| X Magazine | 150 | | 50 | 50 | 50 | 50 |
| Y Magazine | | 30 | 30 | | 30 | 30 |
| Z Magazine | | | | 60 | 60 | 60 |
| | | | | | | |
| **Exhibits** | | | | | | |
| ICN Show | | 400 | | | | |
| MDG Show | | | 250 | | | |
| Seebite Show | | | | | 450 | |
| OB Show | | | | | | 350 |
| | | | | | | |
| **PR** | | | | | | |
| Product W | 30 | 30 | 30 | | | |
| Product X | | 30 | 30 | 30 | | |
| Product Y | | | | 30 | 30 | 30 |
| Product Z | | | | | | 30 |
| | | | | | | |
| **Direct Mail** | | | | | | |
| Q1 Launch | 250 | 75 | | | | |
| Q2 Launch | | | | 250 | 75 | |
| | | | | | | |
| **Online** | | | | | | |
| Google | 25 | 25 | 25 | 25 | 25 | 25 |
| MSN | 40 | 40 | 40 | 40 | 40 | 40 |
| Yahoo | 40 | 40 | 40 | 40 | 40 | 40 |
| | | | | | | |
| **Online Seminars** | | | | | | |
| Q1 | | | 400 | | | |
| Q2 | | | | | | 400 |
| | | | | | | |
| Home page Web forms | 300 | 300 | 300 | 300 | 300 | 300 |
| | | | | | | |
| Total Inquiries | 835 | 970 | 945 | 1075 | 1100 | 1355 |
| Quarterly Count | | | 2750 | | | 3530 |

Average Monthly Inquiries: 1046

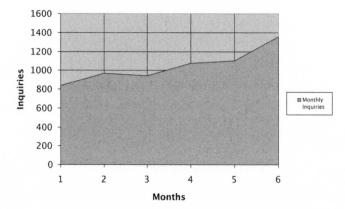

Monthly Inquiries

has in a given month, quarter, or year. Marketing must know the quotas and let their promotional action be guided by the numbers required to make quota. Nothing else matters because if no one is making quota there won't be any products to manage.

2. If you are in sales, is marketing producing enough inquires/leads for you to consistently make quotas? How many products do you have to sell each month and how many inquiries are you getting to do the job?

3. Is marketing properly finding the total available market so that the salespeople can efficiently make quota?

4. Are inquiries arriving on a measured, methodical schedule that parallels the sales ramp for new sales?

## NOTES

[1] Claude Hopkins, *Scientific Advertising* (1923), page 7. Copies of *Scientific Advertising* are offered free from CarlGalletti.com. Also by Hopkins, *Scientific Advertising and My Life in Advertising* (New York: McGraw-Hill, 1966).

[2] Sergio Zyman, Formula for Marketing in the 21st Century," for Better Management.com, from Knowledge At Emory, Nov. 2, 2005.

# 13 Hot Inquiry Sources: Telemarking and Trade Shows

It has been established: One source of inquiries is not enough for most companies. In Chapter 9, I covered the different points of entry into a company. I touched on the handling of advertising, public relations, direct mail, and seminar inquiries. Telemarketing and trade shows were touched upon, but because of their special nature, I wanted discuss them separately.

## Telemarketing Uses: Benefits for Marketing and Sales

This much-maligned, but ever persistent telemarketing function can play several significant roles in lead generation and inquiry management. Telemarketing can turn results in days, not months. Results are measurable and manageable. With telemarketing there are few places to hide if things do not go well.

In recent years the term *telemarketing* has morphed into the term *contact center*, as the duties of the telemarketer have expanded. Telemarketing has split and grown into inside sales departments and help desks. Telemarketing is no longer simply inbound or outbound calling; it has many, many customer/ prospect-facing functions to further the success of your business. It may be managed inside or outside of your company, in the country or at strategic places around the world to ensure 24-hour around the world coverage.

The telephone is not just another source of inquiries. It also is a source derived from other sources that have generated the call (advertisements, direct mail, Web, PR, etc.). Telemarketing is:

- Inbound call acceptance. This can be toll-free or toll calls.
- Outbound lead generation. Cold calls can be made to cold call lists or to lists of your customers or already identified prospects.
- Qualifying prospects and appointment setting.
- Selling products. This is often called inside sales.
- Help desk (aka customer service).
- Text chat/Web chat.
- Database cleansing. This can be for existing customers, old prospects, or cold call lists for direct marketing (mail or email).
- Email response. From the "contact us" links on Web pages to random emails addressed to a URL for sales information. The contact center people, who were formerly only taking telephone calls, are now answering/directing emails.
- Event registration: live events, online events, trade show invitations, etc.

Telemarketing applications, in spite of suffering from an occasional soiled reputation, have continued to grow and prosper. Of course, on the business-to-consumer side there are now government restrictions and regulations that control who may call whom and for what reasons.

I will not address those issues: The legislation changes too quickly for my comments to be accurate. However, if you are on the consumer side of inquiry management, you are safe in calling people who have contacted you within the recent past. For updates on the most recent regulations you can contact the American Teleservices Association (ATA—www.ataconnect.com) and the Direct Marketing Association (DMA—www.the-dma.org).

## Inbound—Toll Free

No, it's not dead. Even as late as 2000 an 800 number properly used in an advertisement could be 20% of your inquiries. Today, if properly used in your communications, about 2% to 5% of your response will come through a toll-free call. The good news is that people still use inbound calls as a way to get information to them and these calls are usually highly qualified and hot. When people pick up the phone today, they want:

1. Information that may not be available on a Web site, including "where to buy" info.
2. To speak to a salesperson. Now.
3. Pricing or other specialized information (specifications, etc.) that may not be available any other way.
4. More attractive printed material that is often more comprehensive than what is available on the Web.

Because a live person takes the call, nearly 100% of these leads are profiled and graded. Normally, when a company uses a toll-free number, they staff the phones for extended hours. In B2B it is generally 12 hours per day, 5 days a week. In B2C it could be 24/7. This fast connection between the prospect's stated needs and the company shortens the sales cycle. Lengthy delays for getting information out to a prospect are often eliminated. Salespeople love inbound calls because they get a jump on their competitors. Because of the highly qualified nature of these inquiries, inbound telemarketing calls are most often your hottest leads.

Inbound calls are good for a company because:

- It begins the relationship process.
- 10% to15% of these can become appointments just for the asking.
- You can get full profile questions answered on 90% of the callers.
- Callers are usually immediate-need buyers: they want to speak to someone in sales ASAP.
- Even resellers follow up and return phone calls.
- The prospects are better served: They get what they want faster and with a more personal touch.

The decision to do telemarketing inside or outside is based on the volume of calls expected and the coverage across the business hours of the country (usually at least 12 hours per day). An outside vendor is attractive when the volume of inbound calls is fewer than 1,000 a month and the company does not want to add the two or three people needed to cover 12-hour shifts and peak hours. Many companies worry about losing "control" over the call and the person taking the call. However, the vendor handling the calls for you will provide better trained and more professional personnel than an inside department that begs for sales and product training but never gets it. A properly selected outside vendor enables you to gain control over the process.

If a company's call volume is small or moderate, vendors will take these calls in a shared environment, which means that the contact center person will take calls for several companies and not be dedicated to just one company. An individual telemarketer can take between 1,000 and 1,500 inbound calls a month (depending on the type of call).

A company that has a large volume of calls (over several

thousand a month) can justify creating an in-house department. It can be expensive because you will need three to four people to cover a 12-hour period.

Many companies are tempted to have a telemarketing department handle inbound calls and have the same people place outbound calls for various lead generation projects. Most of the time, this doesn't work. Generally, these types of calls require different types of personalities and skills. The service orientation of inbound is very different from the rejection-filled outbound calling. When functions are combined, the number of outbound calls/dials tends to drop, and the wait times and abandon rates for inbound tend to go up.

In many (too many) companies inside telemarketing departments are second-class citizens. Management in these companies thinks it is OK to put part-time people on the phone with little or no product training. Remember these are the first people to speak with one of your most valuable assets: your future customer. Inexperienced managers will say, "Telemarketing? Great idea. Let's call the local college and get some college kids over here to answer the phones. They won't cost us very much and we can get rid of them if they don't work out." If the need is real, consider how serious it is to put someone on the phone to represent you. They need training, management, and a lot of attention— just as much as your other employees, maybe more, considering the rejection they experience.

Very often, management can't track the productivity of inside reps—a sure sign of second-class status or a lack of understanding about the importance of their work . . . Similarly, too many companies don't know what their "hold time" or the "abandon rate" is for callers. Even these rudimentary telephone tracking statistics aren't easily available on phone systems that were not designed for this kind of use. And if the system can do it, your telephone administrative person may not know how to configure the reports you need.

Just last year I called on a current client and in our conversation I said, "I notice that your advertising doesn't use a toll-free number as a response vehicle." The director of marketing said that the company president believes that if people want to talk to the company, they will just dial the regular number.

"Are you willing," I asked, "to try a no-risk test program of running a toll-free number in your new advertisements?" He agreed.

In three months he got a 5% lift in overall response from his advertisements (250 calls).

The company spent $2,100 for a service to take the inbound calls. Sixty-two of the 250 callers were considered highly qualified and the company closes at least 20% of those that are deemed fully qualified. With an average sale of $15,000, the company reaped 12 sales for $180,000.

Obviously, the $2,100 in telemarketing costs versus the $180,000 in sales was a good investment. An accurate measurement will take into account the cost of the media placement and other related operations. When this is done, you will see that telemarketing has made related promotional programs (in this example, a print media program) more efficient by boosting the total number of inquiries and sales.

# Inbound Telemarketing: Benefits for Marketing and Sales

Obviously the most visible benefit is an increase in market share and an increase in the efficiency of media response. Other benefits are:

- Increases total inquiries. There is an increase in total response; 3% to 5% is a good percentage to expect.
- Increases qualified-hot leads by 20% to 50%. (See the benefits for sales.)
- Increases sales lead follow-up by salespeople (they return phone calls).
- Builds a bigger database of profiled inquiries and leads. Callers answer questions.
- Shortens the inquiry fulfillment cycle.
- Judges communications dollars more accurately.
- Traces the lead source.

The benefits for sales are:

- They get a jump on competitors who don't use a toll-free number.
- Total hot leads can increase by 20% to 50%. If you are typical, hot leads are 10% to 12% of your inquiries. If you run an advertisement that gets 100 inquiries per insertion, total response will increase to a conservative 107. Five of the seven will be hot. If 10 were hot before and you now get 15 that are hot, you have increased the hot lead level by 50%.
- Channel resellers will follow up inbound callers (guilt factor).

## Inbound Telemarketing Costs

Whether you measure this from your inside department or at a vendor, the cost has steadily dropped. Inbound coverage from vendors is divided into four areas:

1. Program setup fees
2. Program management fees
3. Reporting fees
4. Telemarketing fees (decided in many ways)

The interplay of charges for these four items will vary dramatically by vendor. Some have a low per-call fee but much higher management and reporting fees. Others may have a higher per-call fee but charge little or nothing for program management or reporting. Let's look at the four ways you can be charged.

## Program Setup Fees

This can be divided into script development, training of the telemarketing people, and the reporting structure for your program. The fees can run from a few hundred dollars to many thousands, depending on the complexity of the script and reporting and the number of people you will have to train to take your calls (a big variable). There is no fixed standard in the industry for setup fees, and you find that prices vary considerably from company to company. A lot will depend on how hungry a company is for business. Setup fees are very negotiable, and the fees are paid up-front to launch the program.

## Program Management

Some telemarketing companies will show little or no program management fees and expect to integrate this cost into the hourly fee they charge. Others emphasize account managers who will provide oversight of the project. They charge a separate hourly fee. These project managers may also be responsible for pulling and sending you the reports for your program.

Prior to starting a program, make sure that you have an estimate of the number of hours you can expect to be charged for monthly program management. In some firms the monthly management time equals 50% of the cost of the call charges. In others it is closer to 10% to 15% of the project's total cost (a more reasonable figure). Firms with high management fees will look you in the eye and ask, "You do want your program properly managed, don't you?" They will also talk about listening in on the telemarketers, training, daily reports, etc. There is nothing wrong with this, but you have to ask yourself if your management fees need to be so high. What are you getting?

## Reporting

Reports for your program, including charts and graphs, whether daily, weekly, or monthly, will be sent to you by the program manager. Reporting may be included in the hourly fee or in the program management fees or as a separate line item. If your program is taking orders, entering credit card and billing information and shipping product, the reporting will more than likely be a separate line item on your invoice and whatever it is, it is worth it. For many telemarketing companies the reporting line item is another way to itemize the functions they perform. Reports now come from easy-to-use software that produces charts, graphs, etc.

## Calling Fees—Vendors

How you are charged for this service varies dramatically, and it is aggravating to figure out. Some calling fees show that the telemarketing company is willing to take a risk that the call volume you predict will be there so they can make a reasonable income. Others will take no risk and you will pay very fixed hourly fees. Generally, here are the most common ways you can be charged:

- **Fixed fee per call.** What hasn't changed is the general length of the inbound call. The average inbound call length seems to be 3.5 minutes. Instead of a per-minute fee some vendors will charge a fixed fee for an inbound call if they know the average length. This will generally cost you more than a per-minute fee because your vendor is taking some risk, so they will price their fixed fee calls 10% to 20% higher. The typical six-question call script will be $4.50. This kind of call (name and address and product of interest being one question) will include the other five typical questions: 1) how soon they will buy, 2) if there is a budget, 3) the application for the product, 4) reasons why they are looking, and 5) the currently installed product. Keep an eye on your telemarketing reports to see how many callers just want to know where to buy your products. If you have a high volume of these short calls, they will be disproportionately expensive and easy to address less expensively in other promotions (e.g., in printed materials). Taking orders may cost more because the company will estimate that the order processing will take from five to eight minutes (including credit card approvals).

- **Per minute fee.** Companies that charge by the minute will have wild variations in fees from $0.65 to $1.50 per minute (just a variation of hourly charges). The most often quoted reason for a higher per hour fee is that, "Our people are special." Special can mean they are licensed (insurance, real estate, nursing, etc.) or highly experienced in your products. Per minute fees are good when the call duration is expected to vary from short to long calls.

- **By the dedicated representative (monthly full-time equivalent).** In essence this is a fixed hourly fee: $25 to $65 per hour per call center person or from $4,200 per month to $10,920 per person or more depending on how specialized the person is who answers the phone for you. The higher-end reasons are the same as above. Companies that have a high volume of calls on technical products that take time to learn will often have the vendor dedicate a number of full time equivalents to take their calls. If you need someone with an insurance license or a systems engineer, you pay on the high side. If you have a high volume of inbound calls you may want to hire a dedicated full-time equivalent.

If your volume of inbound calls is low, but the coverage must be 12 hours by 5 days or even 6 days a week, you probably want to consider an outside vendor. Compare your costs for people plus benefits, space, telephone, and management with outside costs for the same operations. With few exceptions the "in-house" productivity of inside inbound (and outbound even more so) is less than that of an outside vendor because:

- The teleservices staff gets involved with non-telemarketing duties, such as database clean-up, sourcing lists, fulfillment, etc.
- There is a lack of firm goals for many inbound departments: number of calls answered per hour, minutes on the phone per hour, abandon rates, average answer time, etc.
- There isn't a team atmosphere.
- There isn't a real teleservices manager for the teleservices people. Too often the job goes to a VP of Sales or worse, a VP of Marketing or Director of Marketing.
- In-house departments lack the measures to track productivity.

When you hire full-time people with an outside vendor, you will most often get double the productivity versus having the same function in-house. In-house people just seem to find many, many reasons for not being on the phone. From faxing information to special "research" projects to database cleanup issues, somehow the inside people are half as effective as outside representatives, or even worse, when measured by the number of calls taken.

Regardless of who takes the call, these will usually be your hottest inquiries and leads. These callers must get into the response management system within hours if not minutes.

## Outbound Telemarketing

For most of us the first thoughts of outbound telemarketing is what happens to us when we are called at home, usually at dinnertime. Yet telemarketing has emerged as a B2B powerhouse for increasing sales and satisfying potential buyers' needs. If you avoid telemarketing because of a preconceived prejudice that it is intrusive, you are missing out on one of the most dynamic tools to satisfy your customers and prospects and increase your market share. Without this important B2B application databases will be less accurate, there will be fewer leads for salespeople, the leads generated will be less qualified, and sales will be lower. Email will often go unanswered, and the inquirers for our products will have less information for making a buying decision.

The uses for outbound telemarketing are only limited by your imagination and your need to talk to more people and produce more sales than your competitors. Outbound teleservices are used for:

- Lead generation. This is pure and simple cold-calling of prospects and current customers to find opportunities. Making 50 to 150 calls a day to find interested buyers is hard work. This job has a high rejection factor, and it isn't for wimps who need coddling. This is a job for people who don't take rejection personally and celebrate when people agree to speak with them. Depending on the target and their availability, a good telemarketer will be able to talk to two to four people per hour.
- Qualifying leads. This is an easy task for teleservices people. They are calling on people who have already raised their hands and want to hear from your company. The teleservices person just has to be helpful and consistent in calling people who have not told you enough about their needs and therefore require some qualification before you send literature or turn their names loose on the sales force.
- Selling product. The complexion of the sales forces have changed dramatically in recent years as inside sales departments have grown with the published success of Dell

Computer and others who sell "direct." Selling direct for most of these companies doesn't mean retail stores or salespeople knocking on doors, it means a professional on the phone.

- Driving prospects into shows/seminars. Without a teleservices professional on the phone to take registrations, confirm a prospect's attendance at an event, and remind them of their registration to attend (typically the day before the event), most event's actual attendance would be 20% to 30% less.

- Snapshot research. Stepping into the marketplace and talking to a broad cross-section of people is the best, fastest, and, in the end, most reliable research you can find. When you call into a marketplace, you talk to all sorts of people: those who love you and your products, those that dislike you and your products, and the great unwashed in between. Compared with research done by mail (especially small research projects that base decisions on only a few hundred responses), calling is more accurate and reliable than mail or email surveys. These latter two are often too tainted by the people at the extremes. (See the section on Did You Buy studies in Chapter 5).

- Database cleansing. Data-cleaning or list-updating has traditionally been done by mail, and it still is by many. However, the issue with mail is response—too few of the requests for updating are opened and returned. Doing this by telephone allows the caller to speak to anyone in the organization who will give them answers. The caller can also find out if the named person in the database is still with the company and, if not, the name of the replacement. Because database-cleansing projects usually allow the caller to speak to anyone at the company in order to verify if the person is there, etc., the productivity of these programs is high. Actually speaking to someone who can answer your cleansing questions can be as high as eight to twelve per hour.

- List creation or enhancement. The key to any direct marketing effort is to have the best, most up-to-date list that is possible. Using telemarketing to confirm that the person on a list is still there and to get mail station numbers and email addresses is critical to targeted direct marketing campaigns.

- Text chat. This Web-based, prospect-connected service is usually but not always done in-house and is based on a computer program. In the simplest system this means connecting to your Web site and your inside teleservices staff. It works when the prospect viewing your Web site clicks on a "text chat button" and the visitor is connected to a contact center person on your end to answer their questions.

---

**EXHIBIT 13.1**
**Instant Chat Session**

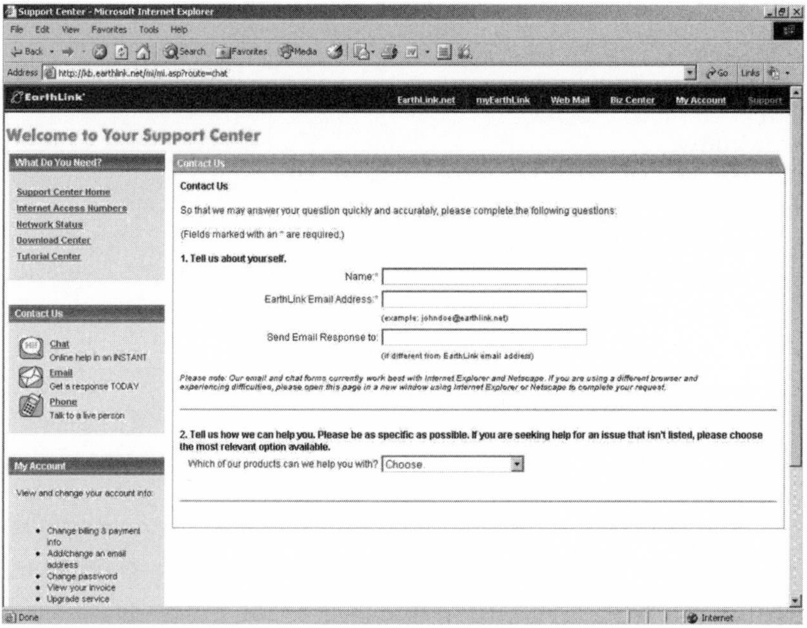

Obviously, the person on your end has to be extremely well-trained and knowledgeable about your products. This is a particularly attractive feature because not everyone is prepared to speak to a live person, especially if they have only one or two questions and do not want to be "grilled" by an inside salesperson live on the phone. The EarthLink example in Exhibit 13.1 shows the beginning of an instant chat session to solve a problem (and it worked very well).

- Email response. "Contact us" pages are great on the Web, but too often the pages turn into a simple pre-addressed email message that you are expected to use. Once submitted, too often the email goes into a black hole and the inquirer never hears back from anyone at the company because no one has been delegated to answer the emails.

## Outbound Telemarketing: Benefits for Marketing and Sales

Outbound direct marketing has some of the most predictable numbers for marketers who have well-defined goals. Once you begin to dial, the results are always visible and measurable. You will know:

- The dials you have done per hour per telemarketer.
- The number of people you have presented to per hour.
- The number of bad records in the file.
- The number of appointments per hour, etc.
- The number of qualified leads.
- The answers to profile questions.

Outbound telemarketing is very measurable and controllable. This is a task where process control metrics can be applied and adhered to with very little interference from those who protest that sales is a people business and people are too unpredictable in their behavior to measure or control.

## Outbound Telemarketing Costs: Vendors

Telemarketing generally has a fixed, predictable cost. Whether your outbound telemarketing is inside the company or at a vendor, you know the cost per hour for every person on the phone. With the cost per hour firmly defined, you can measure this against the results. Whether you are looking at number of people spoken to per hour, number of records consumed, sales made, or leads qualified, outbound is constantly measured against predefined standards. Depending on the target group you are trying to call and the equipment used (predictive dialers, etc.) you can do 10 to 30 dials per hour and speak to 2 to 8 people per hour. Your costs for outbound can be between $22 and $75 per hour depending on your goals and the sophistication of the target market.

Using outside firms for outbound telemarketing is similar in nature to the inbound side of the business. So much depends on what function you want performed, which is tied to the skill level of the telemarketer. The fees for outbound programs are divided into the following categories:

1. Program setup fees
2. Program management fees
3. Reporting fees
4. Telemarketing calling fees (determined in many ways)

Outbound program estimations are based on an hourly fee per telemarketer and the productivity of the caller or group of callers. Most likely a proposal from a firm will reflect the goals you want to reach (number of people or companies you want called), the dialing rate the company thinks it can attain, and the number of records it can consume per hour. Records consumed can include bad numbers and the number of people spoken to regardless of outcome. Each outbound program is different because the goals and the targets vary considerably. If you want to pitch to IT managers in the Fortune 1000 companies, it probably will take a lot more hours than if you want to do a data-cleansing program and can talk to anyone in a company to confirm that the target is still working there.

Regardless of the program, setup fees vary, as do the program management and reporting. Some companies may say that outbound program management is more crucial than inbound program management and therefore more hours are required. They are probably right. As for reporting, the difference between inbound and outbound is not very great. What does vary dramatically are the hourly fees that a company can charge and the productivity of the people on your program. Some companies will say that they specialize in the high-tech arena and therefore you should pay $55 or even $75 an hour for their personnel to be on the phone for you. If the person needs an insurance license, has a nursing degree, etc., you can count on paying a higher hourly fee.

## Four Reasons Why Telemarketing Programs Fail

Whether inbound or outbound, there are four basic reasons for telemarketing failures:

1. **Managed by the wrong person.** The department didn't report to the right person. Oh, yes, by all means hire eight inbound reps who report to the VP of sales. He or she is probably already stretched in their current direct reports, and all they need is to have an additional eight high-need

people who experience high levels of rejection report to them. The next worst is to have these people report to the marketing manager or director of marketing. Either choice is bad, and the department will be doomed to fail. The antidote: Have the department report to a manager who knows how to coach, train, motivate, and uplift the TSR specialist. This problem shows up most often with a small telemarketing department (two to three people) and it is difficult to hire one manager for two people on the phone. The answer: have the people report to the help desk or customer services manager. You can also hire a "lead" who is on the phone while managing the others in the department.

2. **No measurement system.** Telephone systems don't measure elements of productivity, such as wait times, average time per call, abandonment rates, calls taken, calls made, etc.

3. **Lack of training.** The telephone representatives hired get little or no training. For some reason many companies don't give their inside people the same quality of training that they expect outside vendors to give to the sales reps they hire. They lack product training and real telephone skills training.

4. **Nonprofessionals used.** Nonprofessional teleservices people are hired. It doesn't make sense to hire inexperienced people just because they're cheap.

What this list suggests is that you don't start a telemarketing department, waste your company's money, disrupt the lives of people you will hire (and eventually fire) if you are not serious enough about the department to hire a manager who is qualified to manage it.

## Telemarketing and Inquiry Management

Telemarketing requires management if for no other reason than the fact that the department plays a very important role in the inquiry cycle. Many inbound phone inquiries have been originally generated by another media source. It might be a press release, which drove the inquirers to the Web, which prompted them to pick up the phone. It is vital to know the original source and the path that led to that call. If you don't find out the source of the call, which is most often hotter than your normal inquiry, your communications (ads, Web, PR, direct mail) will appear to be less efficient.

If the calls are taken by "customer service," the staff should be trained to fully profile the needs of the caller, not just take the call. Customer service people exist to help customers solve problems and that includes potential and future customers. If the customer service person can enter the inquirer directly into your inquiry management or CRM system, all the better.

Outbound calling is important to inquiry management because it is often the core service for inquiry qualification and nurturing. You can mail and email, but nothing replaces a person talking to a person to find out if they are qualified to be sent to your salesperson. The tactic that only qualified leads that are sales ready should be sent to salespeople has been gaining ground for the last ten years. The cost for this effort is more than offset by saving valuable sales hours. As one manager said to me, "I'd rather spend $15 an hour for a telemarketer than take up a salesperson time, which is valued at hundreds (if not thousands) of dollars per hour in opportunity cost." This is discussed in Chapter 6.

# Trade Show Inquiries: One of Your Hottest Sources

Trade shows are actually 18-month events:

- Three months prior to the show you promote it, send mailers, make calls to current clients, etc.
- The show event itself occurs. Literature is sent immediately after the show and inquiries are distributed.
- The minimum 12-month "pursuit period" starts immediately after the show and sales and marketing share in the touches necessary to bring the sales home to your company. These touches include email, mail, newsletters, telemarketing, etc.

Trade show leads have a reputation for being the most qualified of all inquiries. The Center of Exhibit Industry Research has said that it takes fewer closes (touches) to close a sale from a trade show lead than other types of inquiries.[1] Unfortunately, trade shows in many companies are so poorly managed that the company gets 100% fewer inquirers than are possible at a show. This is because the shows are treated as a one-time event instead of a long-term opportunity to sell. As Matt Hill of The Hill Group, a trade show skill-training company, said, ". . . trade shows are the only place I know of where you can go through two or three steps of the sales cycle in under 10 minutes."[2] The primary purpose of a trade show is to answer questions from potential buyers and capture their name and interest level. All other reasons for a show are secondary. Of course, shows are the place where new products are introduced, current customers met, competitive products viewed, etc. But never lose sight of the real reason why you are at a show: You want to create a preference and an understanding of your product so that after the show the inquiring company will buy your product over a competitor's.

## Trade Show Best Practices

Best practices for trade shows are bound up in either lead generation and collecting at the show or the promotions that drive the inquiries. Following are the common best practices that the most successful companies use.

### Pre-show Promotion.

Only use this practice if you want to increase show inquiries by 50% to 100%,

The companies that are the most successful in trade show selling are those that treat each show as an 18-month event. The six months prior to the show is the preparation time for the show, plus the notification to the public that the company will be attending the show. This notification takes the form of:

- Mailings to recent prospects and those that inquired at last year's show.
- Mailings, emails, and/or calls to the attendees that will be attending this year's show.
- Notification on your Web site that you will be attending a specific show (or a trade show schedule).
- Mailings to lists of potential show attendees within 200 miles of the show site.

The mailings and notifications are great but without an offer to get their attention you will not be as successful as you'd like. Make them an offer in traditional direct marketing fashion to get them into your booth. Whether you use borrowed interest of a specialty item or the autograph of a race car driver, you will have to appeal to their personal or corporate greed to get them to stop by the booth. Do not use these offers if you cannot properly staff the booth to handle the increase in traffic.

## Literature: Don't Bring It to the Show.

I don't recommend giving out literature at trade shows unless you have a very specific marketing reason. Many unsophisticated companies hand out literature without getting the interested parties' name, company, address, phone and email and the answers to pertinent profile questions. Matt Hill of The Hill Group calls people who collect literature "two-baggers" because you see them walk through the show stuffing literature into bags. A good friend, Carol Dixon, co-author of my first book, tells the story of sitting on a bus outside of a convention center waiting to go back to her hotel when she saw a two-bagger approach the bus. He looked at the stairs on the bus, looked at the two bags of material in his hands and then spied a trash can. He then dropped both bags of collateral into the trash and with a smile of relief hopped on the bus empty-handed.

Bring a minimal amount of literature to the show, hide it behind the counter and only bring it out when someone begs for it. Until that time, swipe their badge and get the answers to profile questions and tell them the literature will be sent to arrive when they get back to the office.

## The Trade Show Sales Saff Should Be Salespeople.

Trade shows are a sales event, and yet companies man the booths with non-salespeople such as marketing and product managers, customer service reps, etc. I have even found employee relations people manning a booth. The excuse is, "but we need our salespeople in the field selling." So they send in the untrained to make sales presentations to the most qualified buyers the company will probably meet in that year. At most shows a person covering a "sales station" can speak to 2 to 5 people at one time and turn in 25 to 50 inquiries per day per salesperson.

## Training: The Way to Boost Raw and Qualified Inquiries by 200% to 300%.

Selling at shows is a learned skill and the result can dramatically increase raw and qualified inquiries and consequently sales. Matt Hill believes, "you can realize a significant advantage over your competitors if you know how to effectively work at trade shows."[3] He has taught thousands of salespeople in hundreds of companies around the world. Hill's premise is that there are eight basic skills to be learned in order for the salesperson to double and triple the inquiries they get at their individual stations. He teaches salespeople how to:

1. Engage.
2. Greet.
3. Ask questions.
4. Find out if the inquirers are time wasters or if they are qualified.
5. Dismiss.
6. Demonstrate.
7. Close.
8. Cross-sell.

The point is show attendees, the people who walk the floor, are there for very specific reasons. Within a few short minutes the salesperson must find out why the person is in the booth and take them through the "process." Salespeople who do this successfully turn in two to three times the number of inquiries over salespeople who turn their backs to aisles, talk mostly to other salespeople, read newspapers, eat and drink, pick up their email, talk on their cell phone, etc. Hill has successfully "dollarized" trade show training by showing companies the results in sales inquiries and sales by properly training. See Exhibit 13.2, which shows how a

# EXHIBIT 13.2
## ROI Worksheet for Exhibit Staff

**The Hill Group**
www.hillgroup.com
408.557.8213

*Seriously Fun Training*

## Trade Show ROI Worksheet

| | Number of Staff in Booth | Number of Show Hours | Lead-to-Sale Conversion | Average Sale Revenue | Cost of exhibit staff training |
|---|---|---|---|---|---|
| Adjust if necessary: | 6 | 22 | 3.0% | $2,000 | $9,000 |

| # of interactions with qualified visitors per staff person, per hour | | % of interactions w/qualified visitors resulting in qualified leads | |
|---|---|---|---|
| Average for Untrained Staff is 3.75/hr | Average for Trained Staff is 7.5/hr | Average for Untrained Staff is 40% | Average for Trained Staff is 75% |

| | | | |
|---|---|---|---|
| Adjust if necessary: | 3.75 | 7.5 | 40% | 75% |

### Effectiveness of Untrained Exhibit Staffs vs Trained Exhibit Staffs

| | Untrained Staff | Trained Staff |
|---|---|---|
| Number of interactions with qualified visitors per hour: | 23 | 45 |
| Number of missed opportunities to interacting with qualified visitors: | 495 | |
| Number of qualified leads generated per hour: | 9 | 34 |
| Total number of qualified leads for the entire show: | 198 | 743 |
| % of leads that convert to sales within 90 days (average is 10%): | 3.0% | 3.0% |
| Trade show leads that convert to sales: | 6 | 22 |
| Revenue from an average sale: | $2,000 | $2,000 |
| Revenue generated by the trade show: | $11,880 | $44,550 |
| Cost to train and coach your exhibit staff: (fees & expenses): | | $9,000 |
| **Potential Incremental Revenue:** | | **$23,670** |
| **ROI for exhibit staff training:** | | **263%** |

### Worksheet Instructions

Calculating an ROI for any trade show has to do with generating leads and converting them into sales. This process is almost solely dependent upon the exhibit staff. A well-trained, productive staff will work with more visitors, produce more leads, resulting in more sales and a higher ROI for your trade shows.

Type in your numbers in these gray cells

These are overall averages. If your numbers are different, just type in the changes.

*This is an important area for improvement*

Industry average: 10% of leads close within 90 days

All averages and statistics are from "Managing Sales Leads", Jim Obermayer, 1996, from Skip Cox at Exhibit Surveys, and from feedback and surveys of 20 Fortune 1000 companies attending over 50 industry-leading trade shows from 2000-2003.

**EXHIBIT 13.2 (Continued)**
**ROI Worksheet for Exhibit Staff**

## Number of Interactions

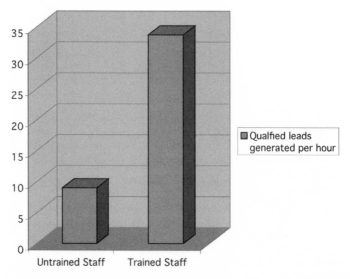

## Qualified Lead Generation

(Continued)

**EXHIBIT 13.2 (Continued)**
**ROI Worksheet for Exhibit Staff**

## Revenue Generation

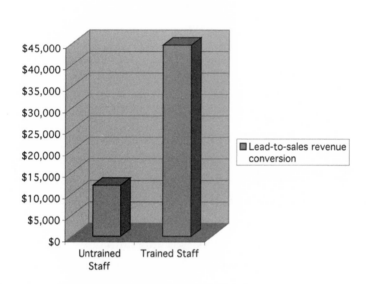

## Cost of training vs incremental revenue generated through training

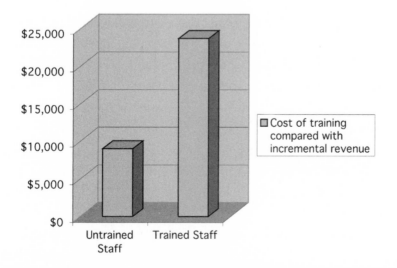

trained exhibit staff can increase the number of qualified leads and consequently sales.

Note the ROI projection that the Hill Group gives when salespeople in the booth have more interactions and create more leads per hour of time in the booth.

## Lead Collection.

Lead collection on the show floor must be convenient, simple, and swift. You cannot expect to be as successful as you could be by having one central lead collection station in a 200 by 80-foot booth. If you have a large booth, make sure you have as many lead collection stations as is convenient so that no one with an interest leaves your booth without giving you their name, product interest, etc. Some companies will place lead collection readers in a dozen places in a large booth. The rental cost is minimal and the resulting increase in inquiries is substantial.

Depending on the system used, you can get the attendee's name, etc., plus you can enter the answers to specific questions. You want to know their need, desire, time frame, application, responsibility in the buying process, whether the product is budgeted, etc. All of these questions can be answered in a scant few minutes. Every show of significance has a lead collection system, which they rent. There are also software packages just for trade shows and also software and collection equipment that can be rented outside of show management. One of the better-known systems is NewLeads, a company that not only provides the software but also the hardware (can be leased or purchased) for managing show inquiries.[4] NewLeads contends that most on-site rental systems are simply created to scan a badge and give you a name. Few of these systems allow you to enter the answers to profile questions and get instant lead lists and reports from the show.

The NewLeads system for exhibit show lead collection (Exhibit 13.3) increases the qualified lead count for a show while providing sales with in-depth details on prospect needs.

## Target Sales Inquiry Goals.

Most companies do not set a target for the total number of inquiries they require per show. Companies that set a target usually meet it; those that don't, don't. The most sophisticated companies have targets for the total lead count as well as a qualified lead goal. They recognize salespeople who turn in the most inquiries and the most qualified inquiries. Rewards can be specialty items, cash, etc. The reality is if you explain it to the salespeople and make a game out of it, the competition among salespeople will carry you forward to the goal. Show leads can double from one year to the next when targets are announced at a show and the results published each day.

## Separate Freebie Seekers from Inquirers.

If a company has a theater presentation or a borrowed interest draw (pull the handle on the slot machine to see if you win a prize), the names gained from these activities are usually lumped in with real inquirers. Unqualified trinket seekers cost money to process and discourage the sales force when they follow-up on non-buyers. If a person attends the theater presentation or swipes their card in order to pull the handle on the slot machine, ask the person if they have an interest in your product or do they just want to take a load off their feet or want the free T-shirt. Take these names, but don't send them to the salespeople.

## Create Post-Show Promotions.

Post-show sales follow-up, nurturing, and pursuit can take a year or more, depending on the value of your product. Because these show attendees have such a high propensity to buy, your post-

**EXHIBIT 13.3**
**Lead Collection Systems**

show program is as important as anything you have done for the show. After all, these are now serious potential buyers.

Of course the first touch after the show is the fulfillment step, closely followed by an inside or outside salesperson. Succeeding touches include emails with pertinent content, mailings for new products, invitations to online or live road show events, etc. The job after the show is to maximize the return, and you can only do this as a working team of sales and marketing people.

## Fulfillment

Literature fulfillment is still a requirement for most show attendees: They expect it. While some companies send show leads back each night for processing and fulfillment, it is sufficient if the fulfillment is done within 48 hours of the end of the show with the inquiries in the salespeople's hands at the same time.

If fulfillment is done with electronic files to a person's email account, wait until the person is most likely back in their office (three to five days) and has deleted the junk mail. Don't get caught in the junk mail deluge of a full mail box. Make sure the subject line says: XXXX Show Info Request.

In conclusion, trade shows and telemarketing both play major roles in finding and qualifying the hottest inquiries your company will create. This comes as no surprise as both mediums involve personal contact and are usually the beginning of a long process to secure more sales for you than your competitor.

## Actions to Take from This Chapter

1. Consider using 800 numbers more strongly in your promotions to increase the number of qualified inquires.
2. As a lead generation device, consider outbound telemarketing to create fast, immediate demand.
3. Outbound telemarketing services is one of your best ways to nurture and qualify inquiries to turn them into leads.
4. If your inside contact center/telemarketing department is failing, review the four primary reasons for failure:

   • Managed by the wrong person
   • Lack of a sophisticated phone system
   • Lack of training
   • Nonprofessional used for the contact center roles

5. To increase inquiries and leads from trade shows:

   • Schedule pre-show promotions to increase traffic.
   • Don't give out literature at shows; get the lead card filled out.
   • Trade show staff should be salespeople.
   • Trade show staff should be trained
   • Have sufficient lead collection sites in the booth to avoid losing inquirers. Set inquiry goals for show staff.
   • Separate freebie seekers from actual inquirers.

- Don't forget the post-show promotions. This can last as long as 15 months after the show.

## NOTES

[1] *How Much Does it Take to Close a Sale?*, Center for Exhibition Industry Research, 2301 South Lake Shore Drive, Chicago, Ill., 60616, www.ceir.org.

[2] Matt Hill, *Trade Show Survival Guide* (Mountain View, Calif: Armadillo Press, 1999), page 2.

[3] Ibid.

[4] NewLeads Ventura, Calif., www.newleads.com. This company provides customizable trade show lead retrieval and tracking software that captures and qualifies trade show leads. It scans trade show badges and business cards and produces comprehensive management reports.

# Rules—Formal and Informal

# 14 Business Rules for Inquiry Management

Business rules are spread throughout every organization. Sometimes the rules are couched in legacy systems and tradition, sometimes in codified rules and language that speaks volumes about the company and its leadership. Typically, the most stringent rules are in finance, next in manufacturing. Of course, there are rules for order entry, sales quotas, and booking and shipping orders. But there are seldom, if any, rules about how the extremely important corporate asset called inquiries should be managed.

My faith in specific business rules for inquiry management stems from my experience with clients and comes from one consulting assignment in particular. The two parties, marketing and sales, were far apart in their opinions about who was to do what and how it was to be done. As the frustrated marketing manager and I talked about the difference in opinions, it naturally evolved that when the two departments met they should spell out the responsibilities of each department. The marketing manager said, "We have business rules for everything else in the company. Why not for inquiry management?"

Indeed, why not? It isn't that marketing doesn't believe in living within a rule set. It's more than likely it never occurred to them. Similarly, for sales, their rules are typically limited to what constitutes a sale, quota attainment, travel policy, and ethics. Marketing has even fewer constraints unless you count brand management and marketing communications style rules.

The justification for business rules for the management of inquiries is simple: People generally follow rules. Once a set of rules is in place, adhering to the rules is less difficult than you might imagine. The vast majority of us are essentially law-abiding people, and rules are generally looked upon as a soft set of laws.

So how are the business rules to be set? To create business rules for your company, first find a person to be the project champion (leader) then get a group of managers from sales, marketing, and marketing communications and a few frontline salespeople together, so that you can get a complete buy-in from all parties.

The most successful business rules for lead and inquiry management are usually one page in length with five to ten rules. A rule must be specific enough to describe the end result and general enough to allow for a flexible interpretation of how the rule will be carried out. If the rules are properly set, time will not diminish adherence even as market conditions and reorganizations occur.

For instance, you have a rule that says:

Sales will follow-up and report on the resolution of every sales inquiry.

This statement leaves a lot to interpretation. Follow-up could be in person, by phone, or by email. A little specificity might help, such as :

Sales will follow-up and report on the resolution of every sales inquiry. At least four attempts will be made for every inquiry within a three-week period.

Possibly you can have a rule that states:

Marketing will measure and report the return on investment for every dollar entrusted to it.

On the surface this looks pretty good, but upon reflection it is not possible to measure and report on the effectiveness of soft-dollar expenditures such as collateral material, investor relations, PR, branding, etc. You can, however, report on the number of visitors to your Web site, those that contact you, those that are an A, B, C, or D lead, and those that convert to a sale. The same can be said for every lead-generating dollar spent on the salesperson's behalf. So possibly the rule should be:

Marketing will measure and report the return on investment for every dollar spent on lead generation.

It should take your group (or committee) only a few meetings to hammer out the business rules and get a buy-in from the individual departments. The list of business rules should be no more than one page long. The suggested set of business rules in Exhibit 14.1 is ideal for a B2B company with direct and reseller sales channels for products that are worth more than $1,000. If you are selling B2C with lower priced products, your rules will and should be different.

Rules are only meaningful if they pertain to your own business model, which includes the sales cycle, purchasing cycle, and the value of the product you are selling.

## Rule 1: Database

All inquiries should enter the company through a single entry point for counting, sorting, grading, distribution, and resolution. If

**EXHIBIT 14.1**
**Typical Business Rules for Inquiry Management**

1. **Database.** All inquiries and leads will be entered into a single database and counted by source.

2. **Profiling.** Inquirers will be asked a series of profile questions that will be used to grade inquiries. The majority of these questions will be multiple choice to allow for easier grading and reporting.

3. **Qualifying.** Marketing will implement polices and procedures to qualify all inquiries prior to distribution to the sales channel.

4. **Inquiry Grading.** Inquiry grades will be based on the most important answers to the profiling questions.

5. **Information Fulfillment.** Information fulfillment (in hard copy or electronic form) will be completed within 24 hours.

6. **Competitors.** We will screen for and delete competitors' inquiries for our products and services.

7. **Inquiry/Lead Assignments.** As much as possible, we will assign inquiries and leads directly to the salesperson responsible for the follow-up and closeout of the inquiry. This can be direct salespeople as well as resellers.

8. **48-Hour Opening Rule.** Sales will open and retrieve sales inquiries and sales leads within 48 hours.

9. **100% Closeout.** Sales will close out and report on the disposition of every inquiry and lead given to them (100%) within the average sales cycle for the product.

10. **ROI Reporting.** Marketing will report on the return on investment for all lead generation money spent.

11. **Retention of Inquirers on Database.** Inquiries will be maintained on the marketing database for three times the length of our average product's life cycle.

inquiries enter through portals where they are not counted, captured in the database, and credited to a source, marketing will not be able to show how much it is contributing to sales because the name is lost for comparison and promotional purposes. Sources cannot be credited. Salesperson follow-up cannot be credited.

Common places where inquiries disappear and never enter a database:

- Calls taken by a receptionist with notes made on little pink telephone slips. The inquiry may or may not get to a sales rep, information will not be captured and given to the rep, and the data won't get into the system. Marketing won't know or credit the source of the inquiry, so once again no one will genuinely know the source of a good or bad, won or lost, inquiry.
- Calls taken by marketing or senior management may be directed to a salesperson's voicemail, but the trail is cold from there onward.
- If inquiries go to customer service and get transferred to a sales rep and nothing is captured, you've lost your ability to re-contact this person in the future and credit the source for the inquiry.
- If salespeople pocket sales inquiries at shows because the inquirers are in their area, that is also a mistake.
- Web site inquiries from the "contact us" page on the main site seldom get credited to the lead generation source that drove them to the site.

Many companies have large points of leakage, where 10% to 50% of leads are not counted and/or entered into the database. By not having a count of all the inquiries, marketing departments appear to be 10% to 50% less efficient than they actually are. Their media choices appear to be similarly less efficient. Prospects often do not get the information they requested, and if the sales is won or lost, no one knows about it.

Designate a single person or vendor as the contact point for all inquirers and you will see the immediate results:

- All sources will appear to be more productive.
- Marketing will get credit for generating more inquiries with the dollars they have been given and eventually the sources of the inquiries will be credited with generating more sales.
- Your advertising and direct marketing agencies will appear to be 10% to 50% more productive.

All of this will occur because you let no inquiry escape being counted, captured in the database, credited to the proper source, and distributed to the salespeople.

## Rule 2: Profiling

Profiling is asking and getting the answers to questions from prospects so that their potential can be assessed. Profiles give the sales rep information about the inquirer's needs before calling on them. Companies that make minimal efforts usually obtain answers to profile questions for about 10% to 20% of all inquiries. These are usually, but not always, from shows, inbound calls to the company, and from business reply responses from direct mail efforts. Companies that are more aggressive and that come from the quid pro quo school, think it is legitimate to ask a reasonable number of questions from an inquirer. (See Chapter 4 for more detail on asking need, authority, time frame, budget, etc., questions.)

## Rule 3: Qualifying

Qualifying is calling, emailing, mailing and generally pursuing an inquirer until the person admits their interest and intent. It is the natural extension of the profiling questions you have asked and the grades that are the result of the questions. If you have a policy that spells out how you will qualify an inquirer, you and your salespeople will be miles ahead of most of your competitors.

Without a qualifying policy you and your salespeople will know nothing about 75% of the inquirers. If you have inquiries from sources such as press releases, advertising, etc., and you know nothing about the inquirer, you must:

- Mail them and ask them the questions (not a real popular option because it takes too much time).
- Email them. The issue here is the deletion of emails or the screening of messages by software. Your email with the questions may never be read.
- Call them. Make three attempts and you'll speak to 60% to 75% of the inquirers. This isn't the least expensive, but it will give you the most effective reach.

The extension of qualifying is called nurturing. Once you know the suspects' intentions you can decide to kill the inquiry, nurture it, or pass it along to the sales channel.

## Rule 4: Inquiry Grading

If you are not grading the inquiry, both you and your salespeople are losing out. They lose because a grade helps them to prioritize the follow-up. Of course, a good salesperson will follow up on an inquiry even if the grade is low. Marketing loses because it cannot honestly look at an inquiry source with any certainty of its quality. Whether you use a scoring grid or move up in sophistication to Boolean Logic to determine a grade, make sure that it is done for all inquiries. The salespeople will appreciate it, but marketing will benefit even more because media-buying decisions (lists, ads, shows, etc.) are driven by the number of "A" or "Hot" leads that come from a source. Numerical grades are getting more popular because they tend to be less prejudicial: Salespeople may be less judgmental of a grade of 10 to 20 versus a temperature grade of Hot or Cold or an alpha grade of A, B, or C.

## Rule 5 : Information Fulfillment

Electronic files are gaining ground as a way to avoid the inconvenience and printing and distribution costs of printed literature, but companies are finding that some printed literature for certain types of material, such as semi-confidential specifications, etc., is still needed. Regardless of what you decide to send as further information to educate and inform the prospect, do it quickly. Electronic downloading can take minutes, while mailed literature can arrive in three to five days (though sometimes it unintentionally takes months). As a test, go to your Web site and your 800 number (if you have one) and ask for literature. See how long it takes to arrive and review what has been sent. In addition, ask for literature from your competitors. When you put your name and address on the request, find a place to enter the date as a series of numbers so that you'll know when you asked for the literature. Compare the "secret date" with the date you received the information.

## Rule 6: Competitors

Screening for competitors and deleting their requests makes good business sense. Of course, if they want the information, they probably will find a way, but screening for the company name (and the variations) isn't that difficult. Some people will say, "Gee, it's not worth the effort." If saving a few hundred or even thousand so dollars a year is worth it to you, do it. Between the labor and the contents of literature packages, you will probably save $10 to $15 for every name you delete. Plus, once someone is on your mail list through the inquiry management system they never leave. They get all of your new product announcements, etc. Nice of you.

## Rule 7: Inquiry/Lead Assignments

Inquiries and leads must be assigned to someone who will take action and will be ultimately responsible for the disposition, won or lost, of the sales lead asset. Sending the inquiry to a regional manager where it sits for a few days or longer isn't good. Send it directly to the direct sales representative or reseller. Assignment can be by zip code, longitude, latitude, on a rotating basis to channel partners in an area, telephone area code, and even geographic boundaries. Regardless, every square inch of the country should be assigned, and the lead should go as directly to that salesperson as soon as possible.

## Rule 8: 48-Hour Opening

Sending inquiries to salespeople or channel partners who are slow to open the inquiry is not acceptable to most companies. Most systems today (at least at vendors) can track when an inquiry is opened. If it is not opened within the time frame stated in your business rules, you can "pull it back" and give the inquirer to someone who cares. "Opening" does not mean the inquirer has been contacted, but at least if the inquiry is opened, you know someone has seen the potential and has most likely started the sales process. B2C companies—mortgage brokers, for instance—want the inquiry presented to the salesperson and opened in minutes.

## Rule 9: 100% Closeout

This goes back to the Follow-up Rule:

> 100% Follow-up Rule: Corporations that have a 100% inquiry follow-up policy, will sell more than those that don't.

You can make 100% closeout a condition of employment if the sales rep works for you. If the inquirer goes to the reseller channel, you can explain it as a condition of carrying your product. You must state the rule and enforce it. The complete closeout/resolution may take months. In stating the 100% rule, describe all of the stages that the inquiry can move through as it progresses to closure. Regardless of the details, make sure you have a rule that all inquiries must be closed out and a final resolution code attached to the inquiry.

## Rule 10: ROI Reporting

No one can do this but marketing. It is their job to create the product interest, and eventually it is their job to report on the final disposition. This takes us back to the Accountability Rule:

> 100% Accountability Rule: Corporations that have a 100% accountability policy for lead generation marketing expenditures will spend their investors' money on marketing tactics that can be proven to find buyers.

With this rule comes accountability for the marketing department and the agencies it uses. There is accountability for every product manager, marketing communications manager, and director of marketing.

## Rule 11: Retention of Inquirers on the Database

If your sales cycle is six months, how long should you retain the inquirers on the database? Some recommend forever, others recommend the length of the average sales cycle. I recommend three times the length of the sales cycle. There are late decisions-makers who won't fit into your mold, and some will have to put off the purchase until the following year. Give them time and keep promoting yourself to them on a regular basis.

## The Reason for Rules

If you do not have business rules, create them, and you will be ahead of 90% of your competitors. And you'll be equal to your best competitors, who most likely already have their inquiry business rules in place. Monitor your competitors to find out. Request literature and see how long it takes to arrive. Then see how long it takes for a follow-up call from a rep. This will tell you a lot about your competitor and about what you need to be the best.

## Actions to Take from This Chapter

1. Find a champion, someone with enough clout to get everyone to show up at the committee meeting to create your business rules. Very often the champion is a senior sales or marketing manager in the company.
2. The champion forms a committee, probably co-chaired by one person each in sales and marketing.
3. Create the one-page list of business rules to guide everyone's behavior.
4. Publish the rules and refer to them at sales meetings, etc.

# 15 Getting Cooperation From Sales

Mark McIntosh, Director of Fulfillment Solutions for Cedar Graphics Inc., and a long time veteran in inqury management services says that "salespeople must be sold on the value of why you need their cooperation. Just saying 'do it' won't get it." He emphasizes this with prospects and clients because he knows that no matter how well marketing designs a response management system, salespeople and their cooperation, or lack of it, can make the difference between success and failure.[1]

A sales manager can simply make sales lead follow-up a condition of employment. While it should have this status, this policy alone will not always work for you. Every good manager must not only tell people what they need done, but why it needs doing.

The key to *any* response management program's efficiency comes back to the cooperation of the salespeople in telling you what happened to the inquiry. Yes, businesses rules that spell out the roles marketing and sales will play are crucial, but salespeople have to be sold on the system to really make it work. Selling them doesn't mean telling them. The following ideas work in getting them onboard.

## Sales Management: What's in It for Them?

A sales lead management system helps managers make quota. The manager looks at the quota given to the salesperson and reviews the inquiries each is getting. Is it enough? Too much? On the right products? Are there periods without inquiries? How many qualified leads is each getting? Are there too many inquiries on the wrong products (those that do not carry a quota)? Is the salesperson following up and reporting on the inquiries or not? When the salesperson reports on the disposition of the inquiries what is happening in his or her territory? Is the salesperson losing to competitors more than the average?

An inquiry management system tells the manager all of these things and much more. Perhaps one of the greatest benefits is simply the fact that with a system in place follow-up increases, and that in itself drives sales up as the salesperson invariably talks to more inquirers who are serious prospects.

Whether the sales manager is working with direct salespeople or resellers, he or she needs to know how many inquiries each is getting every month. While few managers make quota just from inquiries, inquiries can substantially help him or her and the reports from most systems can help sales management make valuable decisions.

Sales managers don't need lots of reports; they just need access to information. They want to know how many inquiries a salesperson is getting each month. Is there an equal distribution? When they look at the distribution, they think about the salesperson's individual quota and compare the two. Is there a correlation? Typical reports from an inquiry management system for sales management are:

- Inquiry Sales Closure Reports: These show each salesperson and the sales resolution of the inquiries given to them. In Chapter 5, the reports in Exhibit 5.6 show how many inquiries have come in for each representative in the last 30 days and 12 months, and the resolution of the inquiries to date. A quick reading of this report by representative and a comparison between representatives helps a manager to understand why one representative makes quota and another doesn't. It shows the wins and the losses by representative and this comparison is vital. It also shows differences in salespeople's attitudes toward inquiries or even differences in a territory. For instance, why does one sales representative consistently show a high number of "could not contact" resolutions versus another salesperson? Is there a correctable issue here? (Exhibit 5.6)

- Inquiries by Representative and Region including lead follow-up percentages. Preferably this should reflect the previous 12 months. (Exhibit 5.6)
- Sold vs. Lost to Competitors: This can be created by representative, by product, by source and source type. (Exhibit 5.9)
- Inquiries by Region, Follow-up: this shows the performance by sales office; a little competition doesn't hurt. (Exhibit 5.7)
- Lists of inquiries that are open. Management likes access to open inquiry lists. When visiting with resellers the list of inquiries is valuable. Going through the list to understand deal status helps the manager and the salesperson. The list of lost sales and the reasons are invaluable.

These reports are basic and should be easily available from your CRM system. However, less sophisticated contact management and sales force automation systems may not have the capability to generate such reports.

The first thing on any sales manager's mind is quota attainment, and any tool that helps them analyze sales performance is valued. Whether they manage a direct sales force or reseller, give them access to reports, show them how to use them, and they will be grateful.

## Salespeople: What's in it for them?

It was a Sunday morning on the west coast, and I was flying from LAX for a trade show back east. As I was checking in at the ticket counter, I looked down at my shoes and noticed that they were pretty abused. I asked the ticket agent if there was a shoeshine stand in the building and she directed me down a hallway to the combination barber and shoeshine parlor. The place looked dark except for a light on the right side of the room. Sure enough, there was the shoeshine guy with one person in the chair and several people waiting. He wasn't a youngster, probably pushing 65 years old. His hair was white, and he moved with the deliberate efficiency of someone who knows his job, has done it for many years, and has eliminated the unnecessary movements lesser men have not mastered.

I like watching someone who has mastered his or her job and is genuinely good at it. You see it with waitresses and cab drivers, carpenters and mechanics, as well as salespeople and marketing managers.

He motioned me to take a seat and I picked up the newspaper. Within a few minutes someone stuck his head into the room and called out to the shoeshine guy, "Barbers in yet?" The man shook his head, said they weren't in yet, and went back to his work.

This happened several more times, and the patient response from the shoeshine guy was always the same, "No. They're not in yet." The last time this happened, the man looked around to the four of us and simply said, "Ya gotta show up to get the business. If you don't show up, you don't get the business." With that he returned to his work. The four of us looked at each other and silently nodded. We all learned a lesson that day: You gotta show up to get the business. I often wonder how each of us took that message back to *our* businesses. The message wasn't subtle, just absolutely right on target.

For me, this is a message I've taken to salespeople and marketing managers when I speak to them. Salespeople instinctively understand this, but fear of rejection and prejudices about an inquiry's worth or source will often cloud their judgment. In working with salespeople I have found that they are cooperative if you simply take the time to tell them what's it for them (i.e., sell them). Regardless of what you want them to do, a simple explanation does wonders. In speeches I have given to salespeople through the years my favorite subject has been what I call, "The Three Sales Secrets That Successful Salespeople Hide." I have told the salespeople that if they understand and act on these three secrets for sales success they will be at the top of their respective sales organizations within a year.

**Secret #1: The Rule of 45 says that 45 percent of all leads turn into a sale for someone within one year.**

While salespeople, by their nature, are methodical and disciplined, most do not know what percentage of inquiries will convert in 3, 6, or 12 months and do not know the Rule of 45. But they instinctively understand the rule and its implications: There is a predicable closing ratio for prospects.

One of the striking realizations for sales reps is the thought that the Rule of 45 applies to their competitors. If competitors are not following inquiries any better than the average (reported to be about 25%) and if your rep changes his habits and pursues a 100% follow-up policy, he will outsell the competition. Salespeople understand the obvious result of the Rule of 45, that by getting in front of more people they will eventually sell more products. Did You Buy studies and primary research for your own products will reinforce a rep's instinctive belief in the Rule of 45.

**Secret #2: Great salespeople follow up every sales inquiry until the prospect buys or dies.**

Once reps accept the Rule of 45, they realize that follow-up is not a 30-day issue but a 6- to 12-month issue.

**Secret #3: The older the sales lead, the less the competition.**

This is the one that gets a salesperson thinking. If they have bought into the Rule of 45 and seen the research, they know that there are long-term buyers. It becomes a short leap to believe that if they stay in touch, they will sell more because competitors will have given up (the way they used to give up in the past). So, the older the sales inquiry, the less the competition. Some will close in 90 days (10% to15%), some will close in 6 months (12% to16% more), and some will close in one year (an additional 20%). As you do the Did You Buy research, you may find your own percentages to be different. That's not only OK, it's great because you'll know how to control your marketing spending.

## The Importance of Ease of Use

Salespeople often have several systems that they must access and work several systems in order to do their job. The system might be for inquiry management, contact management, CRM, sales forecasting, order entry, customer service, etc. Whatever the system, make sure it is easy to use by including a review by salespeople. Ease of use for salespeople means being able to:

- Retrieve inquiries and report back on the lead distribution with a few clicks.
- Send preconceived letters from the system to their prospects.
- See who else has inquired from the same company over time.
- Brag about the sales they are making.

- Keep rudimentary notes to remind them about previous conversations.

If sales reps can pick up their leads with a few clicks, report back with a few clicks, and be done with it, you will have a winner.

## Training Salespeople: The Ongoing, Never-Ending Job

Proselytizing about the value of the inquiry is not a one-time job for marketing and sales management. The first appeal can be made to self-interest, but the process must continue at sales meetings, when the sales manager travels with the rep, etc.

Pointing to the salespeople and regions with the highest follow-up is a good way to appeal to sales reps' competitive nature. No one likes to be last.

## Showing the Cost of the Inquiry

If you can demonstrate to the salesperson that you are giving them 25 inquiries a month and the average cost of an inquiry is $75 ($1,875 a month, $22,500 a year), their guilt in not following up on costly inquiries sways many of them to make an effort.

The initial training for all salespeople (outside and inside) must be comprehensive and detailed, including information about how to retrieve leads and report on them. Reps usually need retraining and reinforcement of the business rules at sales meetings, national sales meetings, and from their managers. Inside salespeople must be treated with the same training consistency as those outside. This might seem obvious, but in many companies inside salespeople get little or no training.

Salespeople must be sold on whatever system and process you

decide to use. Sales managers have to be sold and shown how to get reports, what reports they will receive each month, and how to use those reports to make decisions. Buying software or hiring a vendor isn't the end; it's just the beginning.

## Actions to Take from This Chapter

1. What's in it for them? Making quota and maximizing the compensation plan? Getting management off of their back? Appeal to their self-interest.
2. Meet with sales management and tell them why you need their cooperation. Tell them what's in it for them. Get personal. Their incomes depend on how well you can convince them to cooperate with you on reporting on the final disposition of an inquiry.
3. Meet with the salespeople and talk about success stories. Usually your best salespeople have this already figured out; use them as examples.
4. Create some competition between salespeople and regional sales offices by reporting on the follow-up percentage by person or office.
5. Train the salespeople on your system and then do it again at every opportunity.

## *NOTE*

[1] Mark McIntosh, Best Practices Marketing Workshop, Vantage Point (direct marketing agency), Greenville, NC.

# 16 How to Keep Things Dynamic and Proactive

Because inquires and leads decay at a predictable rate, you now need a plan to stop that irritating odor that persists in the marketing and sales departments. This is the shortest chapter in the book, but it may be the most helpful. It is divided into three steps:

**Step One:** Benchmark your current follow-up and closing percentage. It lets you know the size of your problem and the opportunity.

**Step Two:** Perform an Inquiry Handling Audit. The answers to the audit questions will help you uncover the issues that have to be fixed in Step Three.

**Step Three:** Create a Road Map to Fix the Problems. Follow the twelve- steps outlined in this section to gain control of your marketing and sales processes.

## Step One: Benchmark Your Current Follow-up and Closing Percentage

To begin this journey of improvement, benchmark where you are today. If you do not have the answers, that is an answer in itself.

Answer the questions to the best of your ability. If you don't know the answer, enter N/A for not available:

1. How many inquiries is the company getting?
    a. Each month ____
    b. Each year _____
2. What percentage is qualified or unqualified?
    a. Qualified___
    b. Unqualified ___
3. What percentage of inquiries is:
    a. Followed up ___ %
    b. Resolved    ___ %
4. How many inquiries is each salesperson/channel partner/ reseller getting?
    a. Per year ____
    b. Per month ___
5. What percentage of inquiries is closing?
    a. For you ___%
    b. For your competitors ___%
    c. By product ___%
6. For which lead generation sources are you measuring the return on investment?
    a. Print advertising ___
    b. Online advertising ___
    c. Public relations ___
    d. Direct mail ___
    e. Outbound telemarketing ___
    f. Web seminars ___
    g. Live seminars ___
    h. Trade shows ___
    i. Search engine optimization ___
    j. TV ___

7. Chart the inquiries received each month:
   a. By product ____
   b. By salesperson ____
8. Are there substantial dips in inquiries (brownouts) or a total stoppage of inquiries (blackouts)?
   Yes ____ What happens?_____
   No ____

In addition to knowing the quantity and quality of sales inquiries, you should also understand how you are currently managing inquiries.

## Step Two: Perform an Inquiry Handling Audit

1. What department is responsible for inquiry management? Is marketing or marketing communications responsible for managing the sales lead process or is it sales? Who is doing it?
   a. Marketing _____
   b. Marketing Communications _____
   c. Sales or sales operations _____
2. Are there business rules to live by?
   Do business rules exist for managing the inquiry, sales follow-up, and ROI reporting? Don't make a judgment yet; just find out if the rules exist.
   _____ Yes _____ No
3. Data Entry?
   a. Who does the data entry? _____
   b. How often is it done? _____
   c. How long does it take to get an inquiry to a salesperson?
      • Hours _____
      • 1 day _____

- 2 days _____
- A weekor longer? _____

4. Are competitors screened out?

Are you wasting money sending literature to competitors?

_____ Yes _____ No

5. How soon does literature get sent to the prospect?

a. _____ Same day

b. _____ Within 24 hours

c. _____ Within 48 hours

d. _____ On average a week

e. _____ Longer than a week

6. Can you provide e-fulfillment?

Eliminating printed literature is the hue and cry of many marketing departments. Can you replace any of the printed literature with PDF electronic representations of your literature?

_____ Yes _____ No

7. How do you handle duplicates?

_____ Ignore them

_____ Send them another package

8. What is a duplicate? You can't call it a duplicate if it is the same company and person but a different product.

a. What is the response to the person who inquires twice in a short period of time?

- ____ Call them
- ____ Send them a letter
- ____ Send them an email
- ____ Send them another fulfillment package
- ____ Just let the salesperson know

b. Do you ignore them the second time if the inquiry is:

- ____ Within two weeks?
- ____ Within one month?

9. Where do you send the inquiries and leads?
   a. _____ Direct to salespeople for the company
   b. _____ Direct to salespeople who forward them to re-sellers
   c. _____ To our inside sales department and also to out-side sales
   d. _____ Some inquiries to the resellers, some to the in-side sales department and some to our outside salespeople.
   e. _____ To an inside or outside (vendor) lead qualifica-tion department and then through item a–d above.
   f. _____ Directly to resellers

10. How do the salespeople receive their inquiries?
   a. _____ Through the SFA or CRM program
   b. _____ By email
   c. _____ In a spreadsheet
   d. _____ By fax
   e. _____ From an inquiry management vendor on the Internet

11. How does the reseller receive their inquiries?
   a. _____ Through the SFA or CRM program
   b. _____ By email
   c. _____ In a spreadsheet
   d. _____ By fax
   e. _____ From an inquiry management vendor on the Internet

12. Is there a round-trip mechanism?
   a. How do salespeople report on the disposition of an inquiry?
   • _____ Spreadsheet
   • _____ Fax
   • _____ Email

- \_\_\_\_ ASP or licensed software product such as SFA, Contact Management or a CRM system

b. Can you tabulate responses?

Yes \_\_\_ No \_\_\_

13. If you ask the salespeople, "How easy is it to use our system of lead distribution?," what percentage will say:

a. It is easy! \_\_\_%

b. Not very difficult! \_\_\_%

c. Not very easy! \_\_\_%

d. Difficult to use! \_\_\_%

14. Are you asking profile questions?

a. Are you profiling 50% to 65% of the people who come to you through your promotions?

Yes \_\_\_

No \_\_\_ If no, what percent? \_\_\_%

b. Are you asking questions regarding:

- \_\_\_\_ application
- \_\_\_\_ need
- \_\_\_\_ desire
- \_\_\_\_ inquirer's position and buying authority
- \_\_\_\_ time frame for purchase

c. Are the answers captured in the database for retrieval and comparison purposes?

Yes \_\_\_          No \_\_\_

15. Are you grading inquiries?

Is marketing able to place a grade on an inquiry based on the answers to the profile questions?

Yes \_\_\_          No \_\_\_

16. Do you track and show previous inquirers?

When an inquiry comes in, the salesperson who is assigned to it should know if anyone else at that same company address has inquired in the past.

\_\_\_ Yes \_\_\_ No

17. Can you identify key accounts (such as existing customers, grandfathered accounts, or national accounts that must be assigned to a particular salesperson) and assign them to the right sales person?

___ Yes ___ No

18. What reports are you getting from your current response management system?

___ Monthly report by product

___ Monthly report by sales representative

___ Monthly report by source

___ Monthly report by source type

___ Campaign reports showing the ROI as a percentage return for each campaign

19. a. Who takes your inbound calls?

   • Inside sales _____

   • Customer service ___

   • Help desk ___

   • Marketing ___

   • Reception___

   b. How many calls do you get per month? _____

   c. Are you getting answers to profile questions when they call?

   Yes ___    No ___

20. Do your inquiries need nurturing?

___ Yes ___ No

21. If you nurture, how is it done?

___ Telephone

___ Email

___ Mail

___ All of the above

22. Do you send unqualified inquiries to your sales channel?

___ Yes ___ No

## Step Three: Create a Road Map to Fix the Problems

If you do not like the outcome of your survey:

1. **Find a champion.**

   Find someone in the sales and marketing ranks who both sides respect and who likes a challenge. It has to be someone who has authority and is not faint of heart. Consider co-champions.

2. **Get stakeholder buy-in: sales and marketing.**

   There should be three to five meetings to survey the current system, revamp the response management system, get the business rules written, and get everyone to buy into the solution.

3. **Write the business rules.**

   The business rules should be agreed to by both the sales and marketing departments. There should be one page with eight to ten rules of how you want inquiries processed and managed. Concentrate on the desired outcome. Give the people rules that have some latitude for expression and interpretation. Consider the following as must-have business rules:

   - Our company will have a 100% inquiry follow-up policy. By doing this, we will sell more than those who do not have such a policy.
   - Our company will have a 100% accountability policy for marketing expenditures. They will spend investors' money on marketing tactics that can be proven to find buyers.

4. **Define an inquiry and a lead.**

   Start using the right language in describing whether you

have generated an inquiry or a lead. When will an inquiry become a lead?

5. **Decide on the type of program you'll need.**
   Will you need a(n):

   - Fulfill and Forget process. If you sell a commodity product that is primarily sold through Web sites or retail stores, Fulfill and Forget may be all you need.

   - Considered Purchase program. Considered purchase sales for B2C or B2B (moderate- to high-value capital equipment) products will require fulfillment of literature and inquiry tracking.

   - Inquiry-Nurturing process. Long sales-cycle, high-value products requiring a close contact sales consultant (or team sales approach).

6. **Drive all inquiries through a single portal for counting.**
   If you can't count it, you can't manage it. You must be a fanatic in counting every single inquiry that comes to you. No exceptions. You must know the source of the inquiry and trace it. Be relentless and you will be able to accurately judge how your marketing dollars are being spent.

7. **Create profile questions to qualify the inquiry.**
   You cannot accurately qualify an inquiry if you are not asking and getting answers to profile questions at the very beginning of the lead generation process. Ask your salespeople what they want to know about an inquirer.

8. **Grade the inquirer!**
   Whether you use a numeral grading system or Boolean Logic, somehow put a grade on each inquiry.

9. **Will you send unqualified inquiries to sales?**
   Tough question, this one. Some say send every inquiry re-

gardless of grade level or qualification. Some strongly believe in sending only qualified sales-ready inquiries. Others believe in demanding follow-up of the A to C (or Hot to Warm) inquiries and allow salespeople to make a choice on follow-up for D to E (or Cool to Cold) inquiries.

10. **Do it inside or outside?**

   Once you know the complexity of the process you require to manage the inquirers, decide if you want to buy the software and build the system inside or find a vendor. Either way will work if you decide that you will create the best response management program to fulfill the needs of sales and marketing.

11. **Create resolution codes that match sales stages.**

   Survey the salespeople and find out the stages that they must go through to make a sale. How many are there? What do you call them? Do they match the buying stages of the prospect? Now you can decide on the sales lead resolution codes salespeople will use to close out an inquiry. The most common sales resolution codes are:

   • Sold.
   • Bought other.
   • Not qualified.
   • Could not contact.
   • No interest in buying.
   • Information only.
   • Future remarket.

12. **Decide on the reports that will drive the decisions you will have to make.**

   Before you buy the software or hire the vendor, decide on the reports that will help you make decisions. Do you want to know:

- How many inquiries each sales representative is getting per month?
- How many inquiries are coming in each month by product?
- How many inquiries are followed-up?
- How many inquiries are qualified?
- Which lead generation source is giving you the most sales?
- Lead aging?
- Return on investment for every individual lead generation dollar spent?

You have it within your power to manage or not manage your company's most valuable asset: inquirers. This isn't simply about the money that marketing spends. It's about serving your prospects better, accountability (ROI) for marketing, helping salespeople make quota, and beating your competitors into a confused mess with high marketing and sales expenses and no clue as to how YOU win. The result—greater wealth creation for your company—begins with how you choose to manage the future: The suspects who turn into prospects who finally become your customers.

# Index

# About TEXERE

Texere, a progressive and authoritative voice in business publishing, brings to the global business community the expertise and insights of leading thinkers. Our books educate, enlighten, and entertain, and provide an intersection where our authors and our readers share cutting edge ideas, practices, and innovative solutions. Texere seeks to cultivate, enhance, and disseminate information that illuminates the global business landscape.

www.thomson.com/learning/texere

About the typeface

This book was set in 11 pt Sabon

Library of Congress Cataloging-in-Publication Data

Obermayer, James W.
    Managing sales leads : turning cold prospects into hot customers /
James W. Obermayer.
      p. cm.
  Includes index.
  ISBN 0-324-20536-5
  1. Sales management. I. Title
  HF5438.4.O24   2007
  658.8′01—dc22

                            2006033314